Gypsy and Travellers Tales......

by

Alexander J Thompson

Grosvenor House
Publishing Limited

This book is published by
Grosvenor House Publishing Ltd
28-30 High Street, Guildford, Surrey, GU1 3EL.
www.grosvenorhousepublishing.co.uk

A CIP record for this book
is available from the British Library

ISBN 978-1-908596-91-8

Travellers' Tales

Some of my earliest memories are of listening to the old tales of Ireland, how life was then and how things have changed so much.

At that time, I was stuck on a camp with caravans parked up any old way, on an old croft where houses had stood before being demolished. Our camp was in a vast open area with a strip of tarmac that had once been a street, and a strip of rubble where houses had been demolished.

These terraced houses had been built well before the war and become dilapidated and falling apart. It always amazed us how anyone could live in such damp and mouldy conditions. Once the families had left due to slum clearances, we used to root around in the rubble for bits of scrap.

Our own homes, our caravans, were mainly old but clean. Outside, the odd broken-down truck and scrap cars could be found lying around alongside an open fire and a black pot full of food simmering away, while we youngsters played in the puddles, covered in dirt and freezing cold.

I daydreamed that when I was older and it was my turn to go out in one of the trucks with the adults looking for scrap iron, or being on the hand roller doing a tarmac job for my father, I would be in no rush to return to this camp. And when I got the money to own a truck, I decided that would be it; I would move on forever and never keep still.

The children were free labour for the fathers when times were hard, but as a rule you got ten bob for your efforts, which was fantastic. I was driving around the camps at the age of twelve or thirteen and bought my first truck at the age of fifteen; a BMC five tonner for £45. My father borrowed it and put petrol in the tank instead of diesel, so it never ran properly again and I had to sell it.

Since then I have owned many trucks and have worked and travelled all over the world. Those childhood yearnings never to stay still have followed me from the Moss Side slums to the present day. And, some fifty years later, I will still move at a moment's notice.

Several years ago, it struck me that the comical and often awkward situations which I and my fellow travellers found ourselves in would make interesting and amusing reading. Shortly afterwards, we were approached by the TV people at Channel 4, who wanted to include us in the hit programme, My Big Fat Gypsy Wedding.

Encouraged by seeing my children and grandchildren in the series, and the programme's amazing popularity, I decided to write this book.

Alexander J Thompson

Introduction

I knew that I had a story to tell, I just wasn't sure how to explain it.

How can you possibly go to work every day and get into so many scrapes?

Things get funny, sometimes scary, out of hand even.

Sometimes dangerous, often exciting.

Totally different each day, and that's the way I like it.

Somehow we manage to create the situations, and yet we do not know what will happen next.

And all of this is on top of living in trailers and everything that goes with it.

With life on the road, being moved on by the police, discovering new places, there is always a lot going on here.

I have travelled a lot. I have been to many places.

And I have seen some amazing things.

I have seen plenty of fun and laughter, but also great sadness.

Remembering that these are true events, I hope that you enjoy this read.

Some names have been changed to protect the innocent,

And some names have been changed to protect the guilty.

ALEXANDER J THOMPSON

I knew that once I got off these camps
that I would be in no hurry to come back.

The Ones That Got Away

The camp looked bleak. The caravans were parked up in any old fashion. The five families who lived here were going through a hard winter. They didn't quite know yet just how hard it was going to be. The frost hung in the air and the birds had long since stopped singing. At three o'clock in the afternoon on this November day, it looked as if the whole world had suddenly stopped and given up.

Inside one of the trailers, huddled around the wood burning stove, the children were playing quietly. Joe Grundy, who was deep in thought, suddenly had a brainwave. 'Larry!' he called through the window to his friend in the next caravan. 'Come here. I have a good idea how we can earn a bit of money.'

Larry entered the caravan and sat next to his friend of many years.

The two men would often partner up and go out working together looking for and laying tarmac driveways. Not being restricted to houses, they sometimes got factory yards to resurface; in fact, they would do anything if it made a profit.

Joe explained his idea. 'Do you remember that big old factory out in Hyde, Larry? The one that was an ex-mill. The one that we tarmaced earlier this year.' His friend nodded, he remembered the one. 'Well,' said Joe, 'I noticed in the long grass at the rear of the building that there were a few bits of scrap iron lying around.' 'What of it?' Larry asked. 'If it is still there, and if the tarmac job is holding up, then maybe we can buy the scrap iron from the boss and go and weigh it in,' Joe said. 'Not bad,' Larry agreed. 'It's too cold for anything else. Let's go out there tomorrow and find out, and while we are out looking we might find other stuff if we make a day of it.' The two men were happy with their plan.

The following morning was bitter cold as the two men got into their truck and headed out to Hyde, better known these days as the home of champion boxer Ricky Hatton.

As the truck approached the entrance to the old mill, the men could see that the job they had done previously was standing up to the hard wear and tear which was expected of it. They also noticed that the scrap iron was gone. Once they found the mill owner, they were soon chatting away with him, and he told them that he had tidied up the grounds after the tarmac had been laid.

Did he have any iron? 'No,' he said. 'But I have been contacted by the Health and Safety people and told that I have to renew the old fire escape. It has been there for as long as this mill has stood – almost one hundred years – and now it must be replaced for safety reasons. You are welcome to take it down and weigh it in.'

Joe and Larry looked at each other. They knew that it was a nice gesture on the boss's part, but it would mean getting burning gear and oxy- acetalyne cutters, then going up the fire escape and following each landing along the length of the building, cutting each bolt and fastener, then the sloping steps up to the next landing, etc. Six storeys high, the mill was large and the work involved for a load of mangled iron did not seem to be worth all that effort. They thanked the boss and, as they parted, he wished them well.

Back at home, with the ground frozen solid, it was not possible to go out and look for any work. After a couple more days of this, and the money running very low, once again Joe called out to Larry. 'Let's go back to that factory and just get the easy bits of scrap off the fire escape. The first pull-down ladder should be easy to cut off with a hacksaw, and the old railings are hanging off,' he said. 'We should at least get something, which is better than sitting here freezing.' Again they agreed, and they set off the next morning to the old mill.

As they drove into the lane, they were moving quite slowly. Something was different, things seemed odd. As they got nearer, they noticed little gold dots all over the side of the large building. The gold dots were running in straight lines along the brickwork. 'What is this?' they thought. By chance the boss was walking out to his car and spotted the two men. 'Good morning,' he said. Joe and Larry asked what the dots were all about. 'Well,' he explained, 'about an hour after you left me last week, a couple of lads came here in a pick-up truck and basically asked the same as you did for any old scrap. I told them to take the fire escape otherwise it would have cost me money to have it shifted by the people who are fitting the new one. They got straight on it and now it's gone.'

'But what are the gold dots?' asked Joe. 'Well, this used to be a brass foundry originally,' the boss said, 'and they found it cheaper in those days to make their own fire escape, brass rivets, foot plates and all. Over the years it had all turned black. Those lads worked very hard here for three days solid. I was pleased for them, and they told me as they left that they weighed-in thirty tons in total.'

Standing there listening to all of this, Joe was devastated and could not speak, while Larry just felt like breaking down and crying. The two got back into the truck and drove to the first pub and got blind drunk. They had missed a fortune, thirty tons of solid, pure brass; the weigh-in of a lifetime.

The blazing fury of their wives once they got back home just added to their misery, and they did not know what the heck to do with themselves for days. That sure was a bad start to a cruel winter!

That was a long tough winter

The Ones That
Got Away... Pt 2

'Shall we call it a night?' someone said.

'Before we go, tell us again the story of you and Old Joe, you know the one with you and Wigan Joe and the car,' Michael said to Larry. He knew the story well yet never tired of hearing it again. A murmur of approval went around the now diminishing camp fire, but there was still time for this old classic story.

'OK, lads,' Larry said to the small crowd of eager listeners. 'It started like this.

'Your story, Michael, of looking for scrap iron when the weather is bad is what me and Wigan Joe have done for years. There is no harm in that. You have to feed the family at all costs, no matter what. Michael had in fact been telling a similar story earlier on.

'This time the weather was terrible, it would not stop raining and so it was no good for laying tarmac. We knew a farmer that we had worked for previously and again, the same as you did, we went and checked up that the job was OK before we asked him if there was any old iron lying around which we could buy from him. Everything was good so he was fine with this idea and he let us buy some old farm machinery which was all broken and some other bits that were lying around.

'There was a very big shed at the rear of the property that had not been opened in years and me and Joe were very keen to have a look inside. We were standing close by it when the farmer, who knew my name by now, said to me, ''Is that it, Larry?'' The crafty old sod could read my brain and knew that I wanted to have one look in this shed before I left. So I said to Wigan Joe in jest, ''Is that it then?'' with a wink, and we all had a laugh because by now even the farmer had forgotten what was inside and so he wanted to look in at what he had.

'We left the two workers we had with us to load the last bit of iron, while the three of us headed for the shed in question. The farmer fiddled with the old lock and, as he opened the large barn doors, just like in the movies they creaked and the dust rose as the slight wind blew inside. There were cobwebs everywhere, no lights, just a boarded-up window allowing slits of what little sunshine there was through. It was full of old junk. Wigan Joe, as usual being the best man to get the first word in, said, ''You need to get rid of some of this to make more room for the stuff that you want to keep!'' The farmer fell for it and just said, ''Right, take that and that and that.'' No problems, we thought, and as we were walking back out to get the labourers, Joe said, ''Can I have that car as well?'' ''Sure,'' said the farmer without thinking. ''Give me a little extra and take it with you. I'm going indoors for a cup of tea and I will see you in a while.'' The big black car was a monster, caked in dust so thick that you could write your name on its long bonnet

'As we went to get the truck, Joe was looking all around for a sack. ''What are you doing, Joe?'' I asked him. ''Just watch this,'' he said. I got inside the shed first and started to take what had been agreed on. Joe came in minutes later with a tarmac shovel off the back of our truck in one hand and a cloth sack that he had found in the farmyard in the other. He swung the shovel for glory. 'What the fuck are you doing, Joe?' I asked him. 'I am not letting the farmer change his mind about giving us this car to weigh-in, so before he gets back I will do some harm to it." And with that there was no more talking as he sliced off the large front headlights that were mounted on top of the wings. "Solid brass," he said to himself, stuffing them into his sack, then he hit sideways with the shovel and chopped off the chrome grill and radiator and put them into the bag.'

The men listening to this story for the first time were showing all the signs of interest at what unfolded next.

' Joe had stopped knocking all the copper and brass bits off the car, they were all in the sack, and he was now single-handedly – being such a big man – trying to turn the car over onto its roof. "Here lads," he shouted. "Give us a lift, it's a heavy old beast." So me and the men did as Joe said. He had knocked off the cloth top because the dust was too heavy and was getting everywhere, in our eyes and up our noses. "Larry," Wigan Joe said to me, "pass me that hacksaw, please." So I did, it was lying on a bench. And then Wigan Joe got the labourers to cut the chassis in half. "Hey you!" Wigan Joe called out to one of the men not working hard enough. "Do you want a neck warmer?" "No, boss," came back the reply. "Well, get a fucking move on then, or else." The worker pretended to get a move on and asked his friend what a neck warmer was. "You'll know if he gives you one," his friend said. "It's a hard slap on the neck!" As this was being done, the farmer came back and said that all of the hard work had been unnecessary because he would have lifted the car on to the truck with his tractor. Me and Joe weren't bothered though, because now we could lay two planks of wood on a slope up against the side of the truck and, between all of us, push the two halves of the car up onto the back.

'The back half was heavy, lads, with the axle attached, but the front was even heavier with the engine still being in place. What a monster! We weren't bothered though, because the more weight the more money we were going to get. We breathed a sigh of relief as the last of the scrap was loaded, and the truck was full, the farmer was paid up and everything was good. ''Alright then, let's go,'' we said and put the men up on the back of the truck along with the scrap. It started to drizzle. ''Squeeze in,'' I told them, ''or sit inside the car, it's up to you, but don't moan. Joe doesn't like men who moan, he usually knocks their wages down.''

'As we were heading out the gate, the farmer called out to us, ''Hang on, lads!'' ''Oh, bollocks,'' we thought. ''What have we done?'' ''Here, you might need this,'' he called, ''in case anybody should ask you where you got the car from.'' It was the logbook. Wigan Joe took the logbook from the farmer and thanked him, put the document into his pocket and we left. We had a good weigh-in, lads, I'll tell you, then paid off the men and went home.'

'What next?' the men around the fire asked. 'Hold your bloody horses, will you? I'm getting to that. A few days after the weigh-in, me and Joe were in the pub and it was his turn to get the beer in. Standing up at the counter and pulling out all of the loose change from his pockets to pay for the beer, all his bits of paper and stuff fell out. As he was fumbling about, the landlord who was serving Joe pointed to this long green piece of paper and said, ''What is that?'' ''Don't know really,'' Joe replied. ''Something to do with the car that we weighed-in last week.'' ''WHAT!'' said the landlord who had been quickly reading this form. ''Please don't tell me that you have got rid of this car, Joe.'' ''Yes, it's gone,'' he replied. ''Oh my God!'' said the landlord, who was a bit of a car enthusiast. ''You have just parted with a 1927 open-top convertible Rolls Royce. There were only a limited number made in that year; as rare as hens' teeth they are now.'' Wigan Joe didn't seem to register this information and replied, ''Any of that good whisky left that we were drinking last night, Guv'nor?'''

The men at the fire could not believe what they had just heard. 'That was definitely one big slip-up,' they all agreed. 'Well,' said Michael, 'that was Wigan Joe for you, lads. He never dwelled on anything.'

The men all said goodnight and headed for bed.

The Brillo Pad and the Scour

The bad weather passed and more family and friends pulled into the camp. But, as always, things never last.

The police were everywhere. There were tow trucks at the ready. The council officers were full of self-important gusto. Policemen had their vans and dogs, and plenty of well padded-up colleagues wearing their face visors watching intently for the first reason to react. Children called out to their mammies. The men – resigned to the situation – just started to hook up their caravans, which were more like mobile palaces. The workers' vans were just places to kip in for the night, rough and ready, and the trailers belonging to the younger members of the families were a mixture of everything else, turning the whole appearance into a shambles. This council eviction was getting well under way. As each few minutes passed, the momentum started in the ranks of the officials. 'Let's be having you. Come on, move along, you knew that we would be here today. It was all written in the eviction notices that were cello taped to your caravan doors last week,' this smug fat chap was saying as he gave out his lecture.

Yes, we knew that we had to leave this camp, but we really had nowhere to go. Earlier that week we had found a camp to move to, a big field, but the council must have got wind of it and had blocked the entrance with tons of muck – great lorry loads – to make sure that we could not enter the place. So on this occasion we just could not begin to think of a place to stay for the night. The men spoke in whispers trying to form a plan under so many watchful eyes, dogs barked, children milled around; things were not so good.

As I was one of the first to hook up and leave, I called out to big Tom Stapleton, who was working for me, to be ready upon my return. I only had one vehicle fitted with a tow bar with which to move both my caravan and his. So I had to leave, find a camp, pitch up and then return for him. He was busy eating home-made stew, with a very large spoon, straight out of the pan. This was normal for Tom, it saved on the washing up, but he told me that he would be ready for whenever I got back, knowing from past experience that it could be all hours.

There was no point in thinking about where to go, we had done that all week, so I just drove onto the first dual carriageway I could find and took the second turn-off. I took a left and a right and, by a lucky fluke, I spotted a tarmac car park belonging to the local sports centre, with trees and bushes all around its edges. 'That will do,' I thought in desperation, and drove my vehicle into the furthest corner away from the entrance, so that I was not too obvious or in anybody's way. Once I had reversed the caravan into a level position, put down the corner jacks and hooked on the gas bottle, I told the wife to put the food on and I promptly went back to collect Tom.

Tom was a lovely man, more of a friend than just a worker. I had known him for many years. He was a big man with massive hands and could eat more than anybody I ever met. He loved cooking for himself and would sooner eat than go down to the pub.

His freckles shone through the light hairs on his chest and were always visible through his open neck shirt. They carried on up to his face, onto his nose and finished at the top of his cheeks; his warm smile, dimple and softly spoken voice made him the figure of a very homely man. 'Hurry, Tom!' I called as I arrived back at what was now my old camp. 'Hurry, Tom, and finish the food and we will leave before this lot decide to follow us and tow us out again.' Surprised at the quickness of my return, Tom finished up and we hooked up his small caravan. Before I left, I told the folks in a hushed voice where I had pulled to. Everyone knows the routine without being reminded. If you pull out and any police or council vehicles follow you, then you go in the opposite direction to the rest of us or they will simply follow and be onto us again. These tactics were often used by the authorities.

The move went well, and as the sun rose the next morning we were all tightly parked up together so that we did not take up too much of the car parking space.

I had wakened bright and early, left everyone in bed and was out knocking on doors looking for work. We mainly look for tarmac jobs but often take on anything to earn a living. By nine-thirty I had returned to our new camp and went and knocked at Tom's door. 'Come in!' he called. 'I am awake.' And he was eating again as usual. 'Can you lay those big paving slabs?' I asked Tom, and he told me yes, no problem. 'Then I have a job for us to lift and re-lay some crooked slabs on a driveway,' I said. 'Let me finish off this pan of food and I will be right with you,' came back the reply, through a mouthful of stew.

Tom hurried the food down his neck, and started to explain at the same time that this pan never really got emptied. But because it was low he would finish it all off, he said, occasionally wiping his mouth with a folded slice of dry bread and putting it in with the rest. Also he said this was a good reason to give the pan a wash. He would start with a full pan and it would go down a bit as the food was eaten and leave a ring round the edge. As he left to go to work in a morning, he would top it up with water, throw in a few spuds or meat and leave it simmering until his return, then drop a carrot or two into the mix. The rings were up and down the insides of this pan, but Tom made sure that it did not empty so that he always had food waiting for him on his return. 'Who needs a woman?' he would often say with a smile. He had it all worked out. He told me that once in a while he would boil his socks in the same pan. When I asked him why he would do this, he explained that it was his only pan.

'Enough,' I said, 'let's go.' Just as I said that Tom started to splutter, stuck his thick fingers into his mouth and started to poke around and heave up. After a moment of watching and not knowing what was happening, I saw him pull a half-eaten, rusty Brillo pad from between his teeth and up from his tonsils. Amidst all the coughing and spluttering, he said, 'There, that's where it is.' 'What?' I said bewildered. 'The Brillo,' he said. 'I've had it ages. I lost that last night when we left in a rush. It was on the small shelf above the cooker, it must have dropped into the pan. It doesn't get used a lot but I knew that it was missing.'

So off we went to work, with two extra lads for help. First we went to the builders' yard for a load of grit sand and plenty of bags of cement, satisfied that this would make a good bed to lay the slabs on. We then arrived at this house and started to lift a few slabs at a time, row after row, and lay them back down straight. Being a large area, this job was going to take a few days but I didn't mind because I could have a look around for other jobs in the meantime.

The lads were doing well. The man in the house had gone off for the day and by tea time, just as it was time to pack up for the day, he returned. 'How does that look, sir?' I asked. 'Very good,' he said, 'and while you are here, could you also work out a price to do down the side of the house?' 'Be more than happy to,' I said. 'I will let you know tomorrow when we return.' And off we went.

I asked Tom if he fancied a pint before we got back home but he said that he wanted to lie down, so I dropped him close by the trailers so the wife wouldn't spot me and have a go at me, then went to the first pub where a couple of our lads were drinking. They had made friends with some of the local people and were chatting away. I ordered a pint and sat down and joined them. After one thing and another my friends asked me where had I been for the day and I told them that I had been working at the big house further down. The new friends that we had just made heard this and said that if I was working on the house at such-and-such I had better be careful, because that man did not have a good name in the area. Getting paid might be a problem for me, they said. I listened and thought that the next morning I would see if it was the same house as the description that they had given to me, and if it was I had better put my thinking cap on. I had put quite a bit into this and didn't want to lose out.

The following day Tom was not his usual self, a bit quieter than normal. We arrived at the house and, to my dismay, it was indeed the one that I had been told about. I wondered what to do but as I did the bloke came out and started to speak to us. 'Before I go,' he said, 'how much will that extra work be?' I asked him for a little extra than I normally would, allowing for any mess-ups. He agreed and, as he was walking away, I blurted out, which I wouldn't normally do, 'Could you pay some of the money tonight, please?' 'Yes,' he said. 'No problem.'

Happy with that, and thinking that the locals had this man all wrong, I told Tom and the other two to carry on while I looked for more work.

That night the driveway was looking very smart indeed, almost half-finished. The bloke returned and, as agreed, handed over a deposit. So for the next three days the work went slowly, but I had him pay us daily so there was no pressure on us. Tom seemed to drag things on a bit, which was not like him. He kept going missing off the job, disappearing then coming back. But we were getting near to the end – 'Arse to the gate' as the lads used to say, meaning you were bent over working going back towards the gate. The last day arrived and the atmosphere was not the same. This man was in a funny mood, unlike the previous days, and I noticed that Tom was also acting differently.

I walked to the local shops and struck up a conversation with two lads standing around. They said that they had seen us working at the house all week and asked if everything was OK. I said yes, but I knew that this morning something was not the same. These two told me that three months before the shop nearby had supplied a fitted kitchen and new flooring to this property and had still not been paid for the work. One of the lads knew this because he used to work there and had since been made redundant.

This was the last day of work and things were now falling to pieces. This was what the locals had meant back at the pub. 'Watch yourself,' they had said, and they were right. As I got back to the house the owner had left, gone out, and an envelope was waiting for me with a note and a cheque. I was being bumped for my pay, I knew it.

I was pissed off and so I told the men to get into the truck. I threw the piece of paper onto the dashboard and drove off. After a few minutes driving and in a foul mood, ready to take it out on anybody, I said to Tom, 'And what's your fucking problem then? Why the long face? I have seen you walking off the job all week, in and out of those bushes, skiving and slowing the job down.' Embarrassed and in a quiet voice (but the lads could hear every word because we were all in the cab of the truck) he said, 'Well if you must know, since the episode with the Brillo pad and the stew, I have had the runs. I got the scour, and it scratched like hell.' We all erupted into uncontrollable laughter. All the way home. Tears just ran down our faces; what could you say?

Some days passed and I happened to look at the crumpled-up piece of paper on the dashboard of the truck.

There was the cheque. 'No point in trying to cash that,' I thought. 'I don't want the aggro. The kitchen fitter got nothing, what chance have I got?'

Wigan Joe and John Joe

Joseph Grundy lived around Wigan in Lancashire for many years on and off, and he soon earned the name Wigan Joe.

What a great character. Twenty-odd stone, built like a brick shithouse, he had a shock of ginger hair and an extremely thin Errol Flynn-type moustache, which was very popular when Wigan Joe was a young man growing up into adulthood. You actually had to look hard for it because Joe had a red, ruddy complexion, especially if he had been on a bender. For some reason his clothes were always a couple of sizes too big for him; his trousers were the same, now that I think of it. But apart from his moustache, he certainly wasn't fashion conscious at all. Brought up by his grandmother because his own mother died in childbirth, he came into this world in the 20's but still lived his life as though in Victorian times. Yet his upbringing did him no harm. It always appears that the older generation have more principles and better values than the modern man. He was also possessed with integrity and a great zest for life.

It was now the beginning of spring, the sun was slowly getting warmer with each passing day, the good weather was coming. And for Joe this was just what he wanted, because his occupation – shall we say – was laying tarmac, and the good weather normally meant an abundance of work for him and his colleagues, now the bad memories of last winter were starting to fade away from his mind. Heading for a pint of beer at his local, the Duke of York, Joe spotted John Joe – a younger man than him, must be touching thirty by now – who was also going for a pint on Regent Road. They had often worked together on tarmac jobs and were actually quite good friends. They chatted as they walked to the pub. Both had hangovers from the night before, so had decided to look for a cure by having a few more pints in the pub.

They enjoyed each other's company all afternoon and into the evening and, because of a shortage of funds, decided that they would go and hawk off a load of tarmac the following day. To hawk off means to put tarmac on a truck, find a customer, and lay the tarmac for them around their property. Although still pretty much hungover, they met at eight o'clock the next morning. And with two labourers in their truck, they went down to Mather and Ellis in Trafford Park for the materials. Although it was a bit more expensive here, it saved them quite a long journey to Buxton to get it cheaper. Also, because of the state they were in, they decided not to buy too much tarmac, just enough for one or two smallish jobs to do that day. One thing was for sure, they knew that they would all have a wage by the end of the day.

One of their favourite hunting grounds was the East Lancs Road, with plenty of housing estates, factories and large houses both left and right. This road carried straight through to Liverpool; if you couldn't flog tarmac here, you couldn't flog it anywhere. Well, that was the general theory by travellers. Our intrepid duo got as far as Leigh, a small town just before Wigan, where they decided to pull over and start knocking on doors. This was an ideal location, with row after row of streets, with hundreds of houses. It was Wigan Joe and John Joe's job to knock on the doors, while the two labourers waited by the truck for one of them to come back with a job. Wigan Joe was brilliant at this work, he could talk anybody into anything.

He knocked on this door and offered his services with his normal spiel to the elderly lady of the house. Sure enough, she eventually agreed for them to do some work for her. So Wigan Joe called out to John Joe and told him, 'We have a job here. Come and rake out the tarmac and finish things, while I go and get us another job. If we are lucky, we will get an early finish and get back home.' This suited them both, as these last few words was their code for the pub.

John Joe picked up the rake and looked around him. The front door was open, with the elderly lady standing there waiting. 'Hey, Joe!' he called after the large figure walking quickly away from him. 'There is nothing here to tarmac – no path, no driveway, nothing. What am I supposed to be doing?' 'It's the front room, that's what she wants doing.' Then he scampered around the first available corner out of sight. 'The crazy bastard!' John swore to himself. 'He knows full well that this tarmac is not meant for indoors. It is for streets and paths, and gives off a lot of fumes. The whole fucking house will stink to high heaven.' John Joe spoke to the lady of the house. 'Madam, did you fully understand what my colleague told you about our product?' 'Of course, I did,' she replied. 'Do you think I am stupid?' 'Well, I won't answer that,' John said to himself.

The elderly lady knew that this was the solution to her problems. The terraced house that she lived in still had the old stone floors from the turn of the century. The big paving slabs were very uneven and her settee would not sit level. So asphalt, she had heard in the past, was the obvious answer.

By now the labourers had moved all of her furniture from the front room to the kitchen, as well as the carpets. 'This is crazy,' John Joe thought, 'the bloody tarmac will never set hard, too much heat indoors.' But it seemed that this is what she wanted them to do and with the finances being rock bottom, they tarmaced the front room, and actually made a very good, straight level job of it. The lady was overjoyed at what they had done. John Joe told her she must not walk on the floor for a few days, and that the smell would soon go away. She then happily paid him straight away. They hurriedly put all their tools back onto the truck in record time and drove off as quickly as possible. He was now very angry. Wigan Joe had gone too far with this latest shit, he couldn't wait to meet him.

Wigan Joe, of course, was a bloody rogue, but a likeable one. He hadn't really thought about what would happen next. Maybe the material would go hard, he had thought to himself. If he got into any bother about this job, he would say that he had never laid it and that it was an oversight on his men's part. He was also clever enough to go and sit in the nearest pub until John Joe came to find him with the balance of the money from the job. But John Joe was not as stupid as Wigan Joe thought. He knew that if at any time there was a problem with any of the work they did, he would say, 'I do not know anything at all, I didn't book in the job. I made no promises, so you had better go talk to the boss man, Wigan Joe.' So really they were both clued up to any answers that might be needed to be given to whoever. But this malarkey today with the front room was just too much, even for Wigan Joe.

John Joe decided to keep his cool when he saw Wigan Joe. 'What's the point?' he thought. 'It's done now, plus I need my share of the money.' Eventually they found the pub Wigan Joe was in. They had a couple of pints, paid the labourers and split the rest of the money between them. John Joe then went home, while Wigan Joe stayed behind for a few more whiskies. John Joe called him later to see if they were going out the next day, but Wigan Joe told him he needed a couple of days to dry out a bit, then they could get back into things. 'That's fine,' John Joe replied, 'but please, no more front rooms to tarmac. I will not do it.'

Because the work had been found quickly, it seemed to John Joe that there were plenty of jobs in that area So he decided that he would go it alone the next day, load up with tarmac, bring out the labourers and keep all of the profits for himself.

The following morning he went back to the same street they had worked on the day before. John Joe got out of the truck and started to knock on doors; he could pull in the work as good as the next man. But one of the neighbours of the lady they had done the front room for the previous day, saw them. She knew her elderly neighbour had been screwed, and half an hour later the police arrived in force. John Joe never knew what hit him. In the cells he was almost in tears, and very bewildered. Yes, he told them all about the boss man, who was the man that had got the job and gave the orders. The boss told them what to do at all times, he told the police, he was the main man, etc. But it did no good, he was now inside with seven days remand, and sent straight to Risley Remand Centre near Warrington. The two labourers were eventually let go later that day. It was pretty obvious that the two Joes were the culprits, not the work lads.

The news of what happened to John Joe spread very fast, eventually reaching the ears of Wigan Joe who knew that John Joe would spill the beans and give his name to the police. It was just a matter of time until the police came for him. He decided to lay low for a while, but the next day it was in all of the daily newspapers and even on the TV news. By the weekend it made the Sunday magazines. Wigan Joe had a lot of thinking to do, so for the next few days he drank himself silly. Just two days before John Joe was due to appear in court, and when Wigan Joe could drink no more, he left the pub late one evening, stood in the street and waited for a police patrol car to drive by. He stepped out onto the road and put up his hand. The vehicle stopped, and he declared to the officers, 'I think you lads are looking for me. You had better bring me in.' The plan worked a treat. He was taken to the nick, where he gave his name to the desk sergeant, told him that he was a pensioner with a bad head, and promptly fell asleep in the cells while they all decided what to do with him. It was pretty obvious that he would be held and placed in court with his partner in crime in two days' time. And, because he caused no fuss, he was treated fairly, given plenty of cold water and food. The authorities felt vindicated, they had their pound of flesh, having both of these men safely locked up.

The publicity that arose from all of this was like a storm. A local asphalt floor layer gave the old lady a new, proper floor for free. A local carpet shop gave fitted carpets. And the same with decorators, new wallpaper. Everybody got in on it, what a great advertisement it was for them all. The newspapers ran the story over and again, with public opinion divided as to the guilt of these two lousy workers. 'They are itinerant, cannot read or write, but were not malicious,' they were all saying. Our two crestfallen amigos, after a serious drying out, got heavy fines for their misdeeds. The two Joes agreed, for the time being at least, to keep out of each other's working company.

The Man Who Let
Power Go to His Head

During the course of many years a strong friendship built up between Wigan Joe and Ned Collins. Although Joe was a few years older, the two were always up for a laugh; a pair of characters who were well matched.

The two men were out one day collecting scrap iron. This day they had a chance meeting with a man from Stoke-on-Trent whose business was recycling shelter sheets. For those who are not familiar with these, I will explain. During the war years it was very important for people to build a small air raid shelter in their back garden, as far away from their house as possible. The idea was that, should a German bomb hit your house, the likelihood was that the falling brickwork and roofing debris would kill or maim the occupants, even if the bomb didn't. So a small treble-brick-thick shelter, with a steel reinforced concrete roof, was harder to hit and a lot safer to be in, if and when there was an air raid. That was one type of shelter, mainly for the upper classes, for the well-off people. The other type of shelter was an Anderson shelter, very basic. This was made of long corrugated iron sheets, four feet wide and eight feet high. They were sunk into the ground at least eighteen inches down, then curved pieces were bolted to the top to form an arch, with another long piece going down to make an upside down 'U' shape. Bolt a solid back onto this with the same sheets of iron, a front section with the shape of the door, and then that is it – a large, almost square can that was meant to save the lives of you and your family. I often heard it said years back that people hated these things, but for sure they saved many lives during the bombing raids of the Second World War. In London, however, people were able to go down into the Underground stations for protection to hide away from all the danger at that time.

Many years after the war, most folk had dismantled these things to regain their space and the materials were left stacked in a corner of the garden, as people did not know what to do with them.

After speaking with this man from Stoke-on-Trent, Joe and Ned agreed on a price for the sheets to be delivered by the lorryload to this man's yard. So our two friends went on the knocker, asking householders if they still had these sheets available – and they were most surprised on two counts. Firstly, most houses still had the shelters; some were dismantled, others not. The second and best surprise was that most people told them that if they took the sheets away they could have them for nothing. They just wanted rid of them. This, of course, was brilliant news. It was all now basically profit for them, they just had to load the sheets onto their truck and take them away. Individually they were not worth anybody's time and effort weighing them in, that's why they were still lying around.

The man from Stoke-on-Trent had found a buyer for them down the coal mines, where they were being used to shore up the trenches where they dug. He was getting good money for supplying them, and he was paying very good money to have them brought to him. He did not know of course that Joe and Ned were getting them for nothing. If he had, he would have cut down their payment for the sheets.

Soon they were earning more money than they knew what to do with. Joe and Ned kept their business with the sheets quiet for as long as they could, but unfortunately when Joe had been on the whisky for a period of time it sort of loosened his tongue. They both knew they were onto a bloody good thing. Before they had met this guy who was buying all these sheets off them, money and work had been very tight. But now they had a gravy train, their pockets were bulging with money. Wigan Joe decided he wanted a new car, so he went out and bought a new Ford Consul with column change gears. It was a fantastic American-style four door saloon, a very beautiful turquoise blue, with chrome everywhere and a fitted radio; he was the envy of all who knew him.

Ned went to the main Bedford agents and bought a brand new Bedford TK. It had a shiny red cab, black chassis, and a red painted body that tipped. These two were the talk of the town, and the police were now watching them, thinking they had gotten their money by foul means. But eventually the man buying all the sheets from them stopped buying. He told them that, for the moment, the mines did not need any more. However they found out later that someone had told him that they were getting all the sheets for nothing, so he realised he was paying them too much money for this product and decided to get the sheets himself for nothing. As I said, Wigan Joe had a loose tongue when drinking whisky.

Eventually Wigan Joe, as was usual, had spent all his money. He sold his precious car and just carried on the same as before, enjoying his whisky as he always had. His motto was, 'I do not want to be the richest man in the graveyard', and why not? He lived his life his way, and 'fuck all the rest' he used to say to everyone in the pub. However Ned was a little more shrewd, he looked after his money. Once the man from Stoke-on-Trent had stopped buying the sheets from them, Wigan Joe spent some time on the phone talking to people he knew, like farmers, about the sheets that they could supply at a reasonable price. The farmers could use them for their barns and sheds. One day he had phoned a farmer that he knew who lived about sixty miles away down the motorway. He agreed to buy a load of the sheets off Wigan Joe so long as they were delivered to him. So this day they had to collect the sheets from local homes, tie them all down tight and head off down the motorway to the farmer – and some cash. First they needed a couple of labourers, so they pulled up at a local lodging house they knew about. This was a place where unfortunate men, who had nowhere else to stay, would live and try to find work. Every problem faced by human beings could be found there, from drink or drug related, social or mental problems and even marriage failure.

Into this den of sadness walked Wigan Joe. The men had just finished their lunch. 'Anyone want work?' Joe shouted out. The response was instant, a couple of men stood up and followed Wigan Joe outside. He explained that basically he required them to help load up the truck with the sheets and tie them down securely. 'Jump on the back of the truck, lads,' Ned said, 'and hold on tight.' The truck they had was the new one of Ned's with room in the cab. But Wigan Joe said, 'They both fucking smell a bit, Ned, so let them sit on the back.'

Arriving where the sheets were all stacked ready for loading, the men were told what to do while Joe and Ned retired to the pub across the road for a couple of quick ones. In those days nobody cared if you had one pint or ten. If you had drunk one pint or many, you just walked out of the pub and drove off to where you wanted to go. I am not saying everybody did this, but the majority certainly did, including us, and we never thought twice about it. I am not saying it was right, it was just the way it was in those days.

After a few pints in the boozer, Joe and Ned walked back to see how the men had got on. These men were good, the truck was fully loaded, and the load was higher than the top of the cab, and all tied down securely. The two labourers were sitting on top of the load, so it was agreed that they would be dropped off not too far from where they had been picked up. Off they went for a good six miles, then they stopped the truck and Wigan Joe got out to help the two men down and pay them. But there was only one of them there. 'Where is your mate?' he asked the one guy on his own. 'He fell off the lorry about four miles back,' he told them. 'So why didn't you bang on the top of the cab and alert us to stop then?' Wigan Joe asked angrily. 'I didn't like to disturb you both, because you told us you were going to be busy talking business to each other when you told us to stay on the back of the truck.'

'Fuck me, you idiot! Your mate could be lying dead back up the road, you fucking jackass.' 'No, I saw him slowly getting up and limping away,' the labourer answered.

All Joe and Ned knew was they had both been drinking heavily, so they made sure this guy had all the wages then left him very quickly. Now, very tense, they drove off without another word. The motorway provided a great sense of relief as every mile passed. Ned was the first to speak. 'Tell me, Joe,' he said. 'He was a bloody thick one, wasn't he? His mate falls off and he doesn't even shout or bang for us to stop the truck. The guy could be dead by now, for all he knows.'

'We seem to be having our fair share of thick bastards at the moment, Ned,' Joe told him. 'Do you remember that other jackass we had a few weeks back? Remember, we were to tarmac that factory yard and what happened with him.'

The story about this guy went like this. Joe and Ned had a job on to tarmac a factory yard, and actually went to the same lodging house to get labourers; it's called Val's Lodging House for Men, just off the Ardwick Green roundabout next to the Apollo Theatre. Well, it had been a theatre in its day, with the likes of The Beatles, Tommy Cooper and lots of other big names of the time performing there. Then it changed to a cinema for a few years, and then back to live acts on stage. My wife and I saw Hot Chocolate, Dr Hook, David Essex and many more stars of the day there. David Essex, of course, is a true Romany, he comes from travelling people.

So Joe and Ned picked up four men from Val's Lodging House one morning, and drove to the factory where they were to lay the tarmac. The factory yard was rough, hard and very bumpy, with patches of grass everywhere. Out of these four workers, they picked out one who seemed to have a bit of common sense to run the job and oversee the men while they went to get a load of hard core which was to be used to level the ground in preparation for the tarmac. They drove off to the local builders' merchants to get the hard core, and when they got back it did not appear that much had been done. They put it down to the fact that they had only been gone about an hour. They knew that they would be gone for at least four hours getting the hot tarmac, so they took this one guy who they had appointed the foreman to one side and told him, 'Look, we don't want lazy men here. Make sure you keep these men working to get this ground ready for when we return with the tarmac. We will be back in a few hours, and if you have run the job as we asked, there will be a good bonus for you.' They then told the rest of the men that this one guy was in charge while they were away. Just before they drove off, Wigan Joe said to the foreman, 'Do not let them fuck you about. Do not take any nonsense from them, OK?' So Joe and Ned left in the truck.

It was quite a journey from Manchester to Buxton to get the tarmac. If they had left earlier they could have got the tarmac for a lot less money, as the guy there was on the fiddle but could only do it early morning. By the time they got there it would be lunchtime, so no fiddle today. They were now in a hurry, as they wanted to get this job completed in one day. Normally this would be a two day job, but that's why they had taken on the four men instead of the usual two.

The preparation of the bumpy ground was the most important thing, once that was completed in the proper way, laying the tarmac was the easy part. But the longer the men had to level the ground, of course the easier it would be to lay the tarmac. It was now well passed lunchtime and they were both hungry. 'Let's stop at the next cafe and eat,' Wigan Joe said to Ned. 'Good idea, we have time,' he replied. After their lunch they went and picked up ten tons of hot tarmac, happy in the knowledge that by the time they got back to the factory, all they then had to do was lay the tarmac. They would be earning good money for this job. 'When we have finished this today, do you fancy a couple of pints before we go home?' Joe said to Ned. 'I think that will be a good idea,' he replied happily. And so, mid-afternoon saw them driving into the factory yard full of expectations. But there were no workers to be seen, and what they did see put a chill in their bones. Nothing had been done to the yard.

'I do not believe what I am seeing!' Wigan Joe shouted. 'What the fuck's happened here? They have done nothing!' Just as he said this, they saw the man they had left in charge sitting on a low wall rolling a cigarette. They both jumped out of the truck. 'What the fuck's been going on here?' Joe shouted. 'Where are the men? There's been no fucking work done.'

'Hi, boss,' the foreman called out as he jumped down off the wall. 'I knew that you would be pleased with me. I did what you told me. They sort of worked for about ten minutes, then wanted to rest. I told them no, it's not good enough, but still they rested, so I sacked them all.' He had a slight smile at the corner of his mouth as he said again, 'I knew you would be pleased. I have saved you a lot of money, we can't have layabouts and idiots working with us.'

Ned let out some kind of wild animal noise and shouted, 'Get him away from here, Joe, before I kill him!'

Joseph Grundy, loved his work

Joseph Grundy loved his drink

The Eton College
Football Match

The grounds were massive, and the large imposing buildings in the distance even more so. 'Where are we?' several of our travelling friends called out. 'We haven't got a clue!' was the solid reply from me and a couple of the others. The reality was we had found a camp site for the night and were all tired from a long drive which had taken up most of the day. There were about ten of us parked on this great big piece of land with our caravans, trucks and cars. We were all now standing around having a very welcome cup of tea, waiting for our friends and relatives to arrive. Slowly they were turning up in threes and fours, all very tired as well, telling stories of long delays on the north circular road, which is the road that goes around London, built long before the M25. Now there were an awful lot of caravans parked up, much more than was normal. We were all coming together because we were meeting up for a planned wedding in a few days' time. Even though we had a lot of caravans parked, we didn't seem to take up much space. Why? Because the grounds we were in were so massive. This was a very posh-looking area of Eton we were in, one side of the town most of us had not been in before. Billy O'Neil suddenly called out, 'Careful, boys, there's a police car coming down the road!' Indeed there was. It drove slowly past us, with both policemen looking over towards us, but they just drove straight on. By now it was starting to get dark, so we fixed up our large generator that gave us lights and power, the children watched telly and everybody got settled for the night.

The following day started peacefully enough. The children were investigating their new surroundings, as were the dogs, sniffing everything in sight. Several of the older women had open fires on the go, with spuds, vegetables and meat simmering away in big black pots; an Irish stew was just the thing for hungry adults and children. Billy O'Neil tapped me on my arm. 'We have company coming from over there,' he pointed out. Sure enough, two figures were making their way over to us. One was a man in his fifties, dressed in a long black cloak, who turned out to be an eminent Master from the college. The other was a boy of about eighteen. They walked past a couple of new 4x4s and past where our women were cooking the food, looking at the cooking pots in disbelief that this type of life still existed. 'Good morning,' the older man volunteered. 'I must say, the food smells superb,' he said in a very posh voice.

They were both very friendly towards us, so we all gathered around them and soon the conversation was flowing freely. He introduced himself as the Senior Master at Eton College, which was the massive, beautiful buildings we could see in the distance. Then he introduced the young man as Master Guinness. 'Yes, you're so right,' he laughingly told us, 'he is one of the Irish Guinness family who make that wonderful black beer.' The Irish connection was immediate for us and we were astounded at who we had in our midst. One of our women asked if they would like a plate of stew. They both replied that they had not long since had a large breakfast, so at this time no thank you. 'Maybe another time,' the Master told the woman. Several yards away some of the men and boys were playing football. The Master remarked on how well they seemed to play. 'If it were any other time,' he told us, 'I would have loved to arrange a match between your boys and the College team.'

I knew that this man had not walked all the way over here from the College for a polite chat and to smell our Irish stew. So I asked him, 'So Master, what can we do for you?' 'Yes, I was coming to that,' he replied anxiously. 'About nine o'clock this morning I had a call from the local police station to tell me that a load of travellers were camped in our grounds. So I have come to ask you all politely to pull off your caravans and leave here as soon as you have eaten your lunch. Will you do this for me?'

'As much as we would like to, I am afraid that we cannot,' I told him politely back. 'We are here to visit Epsom Downs. The Derby is on next week but we cannot pull on there until the council gives the OK any day now.' This was of course not true. We had a big wedding being prepared and should anyone get a whiff of this, the venue in all probability would be cancelled, as had happened many times previously. We explained that we were in nobody's way and would be gone soon enough. 'I am sorry,' he replied, 'but this is not good enough. You must leave immediately. It is nothing personal, it's just that we cannot have all these caravans, lorries, dogs and children on our land. We have a very high standard to maintain for our students.'

'And if we don't go? What then?' I asked him. 'Well, I am sorry, we will have to get you all removed forcibly,' he said. 'Do you mind if I talk to some of my friends here for a minute?' I asked him. 'Of course,' he replied. I gathered round some of the other travellers. 'Listen,' I told them, 'we really do not want any problems here, OK? Can I suggest something to you all?' I told them my idea, and they thought it was great. 'OK then, let's go back and speak to this Master then.'

I returned to the Master. 'I've had a talk with my friends, so here's the deal I want to offer you, in the long run it could save you a lot of aggravation. You said earlier that you would like to play us in a game of football, right?' 'Yes,' he replied. 'Well, we will give you a game of football. If we lose, I will pull off this ground immediately, but if we win, you allow us to stay here for a minimum of one week. Do you agree?'

'I will have to go and consult my colleagues,' was his curt reply. 'I will be back within two hours.' And with that they both walked smartly back to the College.

Some of the other travellers were a little angry at me. 'Are you fucking crazy?' they shouted. 'You're saying that if we lose we will pull off straight away!' 'Look,' I shouted back at them, 'this is tactics. We need to buy time for the wedding. If we win, which we will do by fair means or foul, we can stay here with no problems. If we lose we still stay here and it will take them a long time to get rid of us, so don't worry so much. Get yourselves a good team together and we will have a meeting in an hour.'

Sure enough in less than two hours Mister Henderson came back with the head of Eton College security. He was obviously an ex-copper, you could see immediately what an obnoxious piece of shit he was, arrogant and full of himself. 'What's going on here then?' he said in a very threatening way. 'First of all, mate,' I said to him, 'who the fuck are you?' 'I am the head of security. I have dealt with people such as you before on many occasions, so get all your stuff and get off this land now.' 'And if we don't, Mr Hard Man, what will you do to us? Shoot us or attack us?' Mr Henderson now butted in, 'Please, please,' 'I do not want this sort of confrontation at all. I have come to agree to your suggestion of a football match, do I have your word as a gentleman that if you lose the match, you will leave straight away?'

'Of course I will leave straight away, I give you my word.' 'All right, the match will take place at ten o'clock in the morning, and there will be a professional referee to control the game. We will play thirty minutes each way. Do you agree?' 'Yes, I do, we look forward very much to playing your Eton team.'

The posh lads had been well briefed about not losing this game. The security arsehole started to say something but Mister Henderson stopped him and they walked off back to the college. 'Now,' I shouted out, 'OK everyone, gather round. I want to tell you something. Did anyone notice how and what I said to him?' 'Yes, you promised you would leave if we lost the match.' 'That's right. I promised I would leave, didn't I? So if we lose, then I will leave, not any of you. I promised that I would leave, so if the worst happens, I will. I can take my trailer down the road and sleep in it.' Now big cheers rang out from everyone. 'Great!' they shouted. 'We like it.'

As I spoke to them my wife came across to us with a funny story. 'Yesterday,' she said, 'while I was out shopping a woman asked me if I lived here in the caravans. I told her

I did, she said that some King Henry the Sixth had built this college especially, he loved the place, he even extended it years later. Well, the funny thing is, that in those days back in 1440 when all this was going on, to be a gypsy carried the death penalty by hanging, and here we are playing football to settle a dispute. He would turn in his grave if he could see what was happening.' The men laughed at the irony of things.

'So,' I said aloud, 'is everyone happy about the situation?' 'Well, not really,' one of the men shouted out. 'What if those posh bastards have a very good team and beat us? They will make us look bloody stupid, and we won't like that at all.' 'Look,' I said. 'The object is for us to beat them. Most of the boys here have played football for years, some are very good. Give the other side the evil eye, fuck them up, foul them whenever you can, rough them up a bit and they will soon lose heart, I can assure you all.'

The next morning saw us all waiting at nine forty-five at the football pitch, our team waited expectantly for the others to arrive. We were all kitted out the best we could; some had shorts on, others tracksuit bottoms, most had just trainers on their feet, only a few had football boots. 'Let's have a quick meeting, lads, before they arrive' I said. 'Now, it's very important we have as many fouls as possible, intimidate them so they make mistakes. We will need all the help we can get to beat them.'

One of the lads shouted out, 'Here they come!' And there they were, all in identical kit and looking very smart. The referee was in a black kit as well, and they even had two linesmen with them. Mister Henderson, the Senior Master, walked over to us. 'Good morning, gentlemen,' he warmly greeted us. 'It's a lovely day for a football match, don't you agree?' 'Your boys all look very smart in their kit,' I told him. 'I hope they can play as well as they look.' 'I am sure we will have a very good match,' he replied in his plum voice.

But behind me some of my team were getting a bit angry now. 'What's the matter, you guys?' I asked them. 'Those Eton kids are laughing at us, if they keep on we will punch their fucking heads in!' 'No,' I told them. 'Take no notice of them. They might come from wealthy families but they have no class.'

'OK,' Mister Henderson said, 'please sign this document that says if you lose you will leave our property immediately.' And that's precisely what it said, so of course I signed it the best I could.

We all took our places on the pitch, and soon the whistle went to start It took less than ten seconds for the first foul to be committed by our side. We of course apologised insincerely, smiled and let them take their free kick. After a few more hectic fouls, the Eton fairies were getting too scared to touch the ball. However, because they were a little more brainy than us, they did devise a plan of long passing all the time, so we found it difficult to get near to an individual person. But once we had sussed this out, we had them. Half time arrived. Nobody from the posh side said anything detrimental about our playing, in case we got physical with them, at least not so we could hear them anyway. During the second half they were just like a load of rabbits running around the field. Some of our boys were now tired of this stupid game, and said 'fuck them!' and walked off the field. We were now down to just eight players, but as we were by then two nil up, we didn't care at all.

A couple of our girls had walked over to see what all the fuss was about, and they giggled at these posh young boys who were all muddy and bruised. I don't think a bruise would get noticed very much on one of our lot. A few fluttering eyelashes were given though towards the opposition and admiring glances were exchanged.

By the time of the final whistle we had won by three goals to one, which was a good result for the boys and me. Mister Henderson, the Master, gave us limited praise, but did not want to say too much. Of course he had to live with these posh boys. But we didn't care at all because we had won. Mister Henderson came over and shook my hand and said, 'I hope you keep to your word and pull off here in a few days. We will not bother you until then.'

A couple of nights later, after we had yet again gone to the local pub to celebrate our win over the Eton lads, we had to get a taxi back to our camp. The driver soon put two and two together with our accents and guessed who we were. We reached the caravans and his face lit up as he said, 'I am so glad you thrashed those arrogant pricks at football. They give us a hard time most nights when full of beer with quips like, ''Daddy wouldn't own a taxi company, not enough profit in it at all. Very working class.''

'So good on you, lads, for beating them, all of Eton is talking about you lot. Even the BBC got hold of it.'

We got out of the taxi and paid him. As we walked towards the caravans, the driver called out, 'VENI, VIDI, VICI.' 'What's that?' we asked. 'It's an old quote. I came, I saw, I conquered. Remember that, lads,' he said as he drove off.

We just took his word for it and staggered into bed. Happy!

Puk Fair...

While travelling around together several months earlier, PJ O'Neil, Jimmy Boyle, Bill Logan and I would all meet up at the annual fair in Cork, Eire, known locally as the Puk Fair. This is a great place to be during August and a great meeting place for everyone in the travelling community. This is also the home of my ancestors. My people go back many generations, with Clonakilty being our main birthplace. The city itself is second to none in all of Ireland, with its huge main streets, many bars and fantastic shopping outlets. It really reflects the character of the people there with its easy pace of life. Once you have seen the Cork and Kerry mountains and the Ring of Kerry, you instantly fall in love with this beautiful place; such scenery takes your breath away. If you think that you have ancestors in this area, you can go and visit Killarney Castle where they have all the records for the locality going back throughout the ages. This includes details of births, marriages, christenings and deaths. Any heraldry or coats of arms can also be found here as well. So for me being here has two special reasons. The celebrations in town are legendary. The Puk Fair gets its name from the Puk goat, a wild male goat that is the dominant one in the herd. Every year at this time the locals go up into the mountains and lay a trap to catch one of these animals. When caught it is brought back into town and is then hoisted up in a wooden bamboo box some 30ft, high above the watching crowds. And there it will stay for five days and five nights. The goat then becomes the star. And this is why.

Legend has it that Oliver Cromwell's army invaded Ireland and approached Cork unbeknown to everybody, with the intention of capturing the city. As the army assembled outside of town a herd of goats was startled. The nervous Puk ran off and headed into the town square, but the locals seeing this could not understand why the male had left its females. Somebody went out to the hills to have a scout around and came hurriedly back with the news of the invaders. Many lives were saved that night through these actions, so the goat's deeds had saved the day.

Later, when he is lowered surrounded in mirth, the goat becomes King and is crowned in a mock ceremony and paraded around town to the delight of all.

The merriment of drinking for this weekend is echoed in the words all around, that 'whilst the Goat is the King, the people act the goat'. The fair has become the oldest and the largest non-religious event in all of Ireland. So much so that King James the First in 1603 granted legal status to the fair being held. Ballinasloe Horse Fair is the only other fair to come close in size to this event.

This year's festivities attracted over 100,000 people and the guests who opened the first day's events were the pop group, The Drifters.

Enjoying all of this atmosphere, we headed out of town to soak up what was happening in the main field where all of the tents and market stalls were situated. Entering the enclosure, the first thing that we spotted was the donkey, yes the donkey. I recognised it straight away. A short black thing with a white patch close to the end of its tail. There was no mistaking this creature. 'What's all this about?' PJ asked. So I told him. An event like this with such big crowds is an ideal time to raise funds for local good causes. The parish priest has one such good cause in his mind at this time of the year – the children and pensioners in his community. Every year this donkey is paraded around the stalls and tents. The priest is always there offering any children a free go on the donkey's back, followed by the words, 'It can be yours for a couple of pounds, go ask your mammy or your daddy. It is being raffled at three o'clock sharp.' After a short ride on the animal's back, the children are begging their parents to buy them a ticket. But the townsfolk put up a weak fight. 'No, my girl, I will buy you a better donkey at the cattle market next week,' a father will be heard saying. The pleading continues until the mum or dad relents and purchases a ticket from the priest who by now is wearing a pious yet devilish smile. 'I will see you at mass, Paddy,' he would whisper to the beaten parent with a wink. The reason for all this, which is going on in full view of everybody, is that this animal gets 'auctioned off' every year. The priest always seems to get handed the winning ticket and gets to keep the prize, so after the auction he takes the donkey home again until next year. The locals keep this tradition between themselves and pass this down to their children as they in turn get older.

'A good story,' PJ said back to me as we headed for the beer tent.

After an hour or so there was a great commotion going on. Down the lane that leads out of the town, a couple of young travelling girls were walking back towards the caravans. Barbara and Eileen could not get a taxi so walking was the only way to get back home, when a trailer full of livestock being towed by a jeep broke free from the towbar and careered off on its own at great speed. The lanes were packed with parked-up motors and hundreds of people on foot. Everybody scrambled to avoid this very dangerous situation, screams were heard and there was chaos all around. But the young girls got caught, they were not quick enough. Serious damage was done and things looked critical, but the air ambulance arrived in time to transport the casualties to hospital. It was not possible for the police or normal ambulance to get there quickly, such was the volume of traffic at this event. The doctors in the city hospital fought hard to save an arm and a leg, and dealt with lots of fractures. Several days later our girls were allowed home and, after many months of physiotherapy, made a wonderful recovery from a truly horrific accident I am pleased to say.

We never got to see the end of the Puk Fair that year, or the lowering of the goat. The day after the accident, after a couple of phone calls had been made, the only words being said in the travelling community was, 'It's on!' The biggest fight in many years would take place between the two most powerful men amongst English and Irish travellers. The fight to be the best of both sides. This could not be missed. It was decided that night that we would leave this place and head to the north to witness the great occasion.

The Big Fight, Newry, NI

We are on our way. Barbara and Eileen are OK, the goat is let loose, and we are breaking every speed limit, all of the highway laws and all of the by laws to be there on time.

The big fight was to take place that very day in Newry, Northern Ireland, which is about one hundred and sixty miles from Cork city, so we had a few hours' drive to get there and watch this great spectacle. The drive, if it were in England, would not pose any problems, but this journey was from the deep south of Ireland. There were no real major roads, just a network of narrow lanes with the odd small dual carriageway to pass the occasional tractor that was slowing your driving down. After many wrong turns and slightly getting lost, we made it. Once we arrived, we could feel the tension in the town; the atmosphere was like no other I had felt or seen. One of the fighters, Sammy Boyle from Yorkshire, stood well over six feet tall and close on nineteen stone in weight. He visited every fair or gathering of travellers and had beaten every man that had dared stand before him; he had never lost a single fight. He had been the number one fighter for many years, but now a very serious challenger had come along, a very hard man and fighter by the name of Bill Logan. He too was a strong and seasoned fighter, not as tall as Sammy Boyle, but very broad and muscular. To his people he was the best, a fearsome fighter, and – like Boyle – had never been beaten.

The fight was to take place that day in the town square at one-thirty, with a large crowd expected. All the people who had supported Sammy over the years were at this moment afraid for him. He was facing a mighty man, and this was possibly the biggest challenge of his fighting life.

The crowds started to arrive at the square about twelve o'clock so they could get a good view of the fight. As time went on, more and more people were arriving, each side here to watch their man win. There was one big problem - no sign of Sammy Boyle yet, no-one had seen him or his entourage. Now it was one o'clock, the ring had been set up ages ago. The Logan people were now around the ring, waiting on their fighter to enter it with a lot of showmanship. The talk between the big crowds now was where was Sammy Boyle? One-twenty. Bill Logan had now entered the ring amid a massive response from his followers. Meanwhile, the Boyle camp had made frantic calls to England where Sammy lived, to see if he had left or was nearly in Ireland.

The information that came back was that he had been delayed at London airport, so it was agreed between the two camps that the fight would now take place the next day at four o'clock in the afternoon.

For those who are not aware, the British government were going through a tough period with the IRA at that time, and this particular town was a stronghold for the movement. Across from the square in the town, directly facing where the fight action was to take place, was the army barracks. It was a very frightening looking compound made of corrugated sheet steel, close on thirty feet high, and around the top was double stranded barbed wire. The large gates were heavy duty thick steel, which took two soldiers to open each one. The whole compound looked fearsome to the local people, so goodness knows what the soldiers felt like that had to live there. But today was different, the crowds did not give a fuck about this place, the soldiers, the armoured trucks or the big helicopter that was always hovering over the town. They were here to enjoy this big fight and nothing or no-one was going to spoil it.

Everyone knew of the deadline at four o'clock. If Sammy Boyle didn't show, the fight would go to Bill Logan. Soon all the soldiers were ordered to return to barracks, the chopper made to go and hover somewhere else, but still the crowds were coming into the square. There were some very important local men in the crowd, apart from the travelling people. The two communities got on very well, probably more than the British government were ever aware of.

Town life seemed very different today. The shops, the pubs, even the people seemed to have a feeling of uncertainty. They knew so much about this fight. This man Sammy Boyle, who some knew and others would like to have known, had fast become the local hero. In fact, not just locally. Today's events were spreading all over the country like wildfire. His reputation would be on the line today, with some thinking he would meet his match in the challenger, so the stories were flowing like wine at a tasting. The one big fear running through his followers was that, not only would Sammy get beaten, but also seriously hurt. It was well known that Bill Logan had been training very hard for this bout with weight training and running mile after mile with a heavy duty truck battery tied across his back. Sparring was important to ensure his reflexes were sharp, and he was supremely confident he would win this fight.

It was also a special week for the local people, when the annual special Mass was held in the chapel of the Catholic Cemetery to bless the graves of the departed souls of the local people. Sometimes, if weather permits, it is held outside in the open air. The priest, having heard the news of the fight, expressed concern but no-one took any heed. There was way too much pride at stake for both men.

The fight was fast being billed as The King of the Gypsies. Back in the town square the very large crowd started to appear again, arriving from all directions, travellers and non-travellers. They came in their thousands, more so because the postponement the day before had allowed more people the chance to come. Even the local toilet block roof was taken up by a load of young people anxious to watch the fight.

The hour for the fight drew ever closer. Two referees – one from each side – was nominated. It was suggested that more referees would be needed because of the size of the crowd, however it was also said that if these men were so good, they wouldn't need any referees at all. The village square was very big, and the question of holding back such a big crowd came up. The solution was a single ball of thin string. It was tied around a lamp post, and then onto the next and the next and so on, plus it went around the bike railings and so a fighting ring was made. It was declared to all spectators that should any man step inside this ring while the fight was in progress, he would be matched up with one of the opposing side and forced to fight him.

Both the fighters up until this time had remained out of view, but now all the talking and bullshit was over, it was down to the serious business of fighting. Logan was the first to enter the makeshift ring to thunderous applause. Each hand bound tight in white boxers' tape, he came dancing into the ring, hands above his head, milking the applause from the crowd with a beaming smile. He then walked over and shook hands with the opposing side's referee. Long, slow moments passed, then from the far end of the car park, for the first time in full view of the public, strode the mighty figure of Sammy Boyle. With a very stern, determined face, he showed no fear, yet he knew he carried the hopes of family, friends and all the well-wishers he had met.

As Sammy walked straight to the centre of the ring, he casually unbuttoned his shirt and let it slip to the ground. Logan's referee shook hands with Sammy and briefly said something to him. Sammy never spoke to anyone, but reached out a hand to his opponent then, with a nod of his head, got down to the job in hand. Logan came forward and started his assault. The fight was fiercely contested, with both men giving their all. Logan was floored by a superb right to the chin from Sammy, but got up from this tremendous haymaker, shook his head and continued when most men would have stayed down from such an almighty punch. Now Logan was hitting Sammy's face so hard he was badly marking his eyes and face. This pounding from both men went on unabated for a good thirty minutes. There are no breaks in this type of fighting and it can go on for a seriously long time; the rules are fight till you drop or fight till you die, and of course many fighters have died in the past.

The crowd was now getting very anxious, tempers were becoming raised, people were moving forward, the ring was becoming smaller and smaller, so the rules of the boundary lines were totally dismissed in all of this chaos. Between wanting to cheer on your man, or not wanting the other side to get the upper hand by fouling your man, the crowd was slowly moving in. There was total brutality all around now, nothing made sense any more as the shouts of encouragement from both sides started to become vicious. Soon, because the ring had now become so small, it was down to toe-to-toe fighting. Both men's faces were a mess, with their eyes now starting to close and cuts and blood everywhere. Eventually there was not even room to swing a punch as the crowd moved in even closer, but the two hard, brave men still fought on the best they could.

Now they were at the point where there just wasn't any room to fight any more. It was really quite stupid of the crowd to let it get to this situation, after all, how can fighters fight without room to do it? Then the fight just came to a sudden stop, the fighters were pulled apart, and both sides were trying to claim the victory. After half an hour of trying to resolve who the winner actually was, Sammy Boyle got back into the ring to finish things off, but Logan wasn't around. He thought he had already done enough to win it, and wasn't aware of what was happening in his absence. So Sammy stood alone, waiting for his opponent, but it was impossible to contact Logan. In those days, of course, there were no mobile phones, no instant contact at all. Trying to get out of town was a nightmare – there was a huge tidal wave of cars and vans all trying to move, but getting nowhere. Anyone who had left town earlier couldn't get back in at all, there were jams in every direction.

As time passed and minutes turned into an hour or more, people started to realise it was all over. The two men had given their all, there would be no more today. Amongst the travelling community things quietened off for a while, the two titans had done their stuff but a certain uneasiness hung in the air. Sammy was loved and admired by all, and I am certain that he still is.

Having his own thoughts, his own outlook on life and the mysteries that surround any mortal man when he comes to meet his maker, Sammy decided after this fight that, for him at least, enough was enough and he turned his life to Jesus. Yes, you heard it right, he has given his life to Jesus. From the age of just sixteen years old Sammy had been fighting fully grown men and beating them, now he has renounced violence completely.

In a truly wonderful act of self-denial, he turned his back on fighting, turned his life around and declared, 'Get thee behind me, Satan.' He is now, and has been for many years, a peace loving, family man and always a gentleman. He turned his back and renounced his former life, something had changed this mighty man. Those hands, so large they could envelop a pint glass of beer, that held strong liquor so often, now held just the Bible. Those battle-scarred hands now gently hold the word of God. The fingers that had held so many cigarettes between them were now clean, pure and unsoiled. All of those dance floors and nightclubs have been relegated into history.

A big man made a giant move to better his life – that's Sammy Boyle.

To Bill Logan, who still fights, we wish him and his family well.

Three Men, Two Fences,
One Field and a Motorway

Back in England some time later, Paddy O'Neil and his close friends, John Joe and Michael O'Connell had been looking at a piece of ground that was for sale near the motorway. They had all noticed the 'for sale' sign at least a week earlier. Even before they knew the price of this piece of land, they had pulled down the 'for sale' sign, written the phone number on a piece of paper and thrown the sign into a skip at the side of the road. The land was in a great position for these scheming men. They had a great plan that was a little illegal, so they were all a little nervous of the situation.

The land was a mile from the village, nestled between a low-lying country lane and running parallel with the M25 motorway, which actually was not a problem as it was a good twenty feet high up a bank. If the price was right, they all agreed that they would chip in and buy it. That's why they took the sign away; they wanted to keep it all hush-hush, before other people saw it was for sale and got the same idea, maybe causing a bidding war amongst possible buyers. The three men had contacted the estate agent, who had told them the price of the land. They made a cash offer on the condition that the deal was completed quickly. 'We must return to Ireland on important business,' they had said, 'so we would like to finalise this before we go.' They knew of other travellers who had also bought up land with the idea of making a permanent base for themselves and their families, so why shouldn't they try?

Amazingly their offer was accepted. The legalities in those days were very limited and soon they had placed the funds in the hands of the acting solicitor – ten days from start to finish, job done.

'Now, lads,' Michael had said to his friends, 'the weekend after next is a bank holiday. You both know the score here. The last thing on Friday afternoon, we will have all the forms already filled in by the woman in our local shop for the permission to apply to use the land as a caravan site. I have paid the woman for filling in the forms because, as you know, none of us can read and write enough to do it.

'We will then take the sealed letter to the council offices late Friday afternoon, as we know that nobody will even bother to read letters that late on a Friday let alone a Bank Holiday Friday. Then we will get ready for moving all our caravans onto this land at six o'clock on Saturday morning.' They were of course banking on the reality that the people in the council offices had a motto of, 'it's now very late on Friday, so it can wait until Tuesday', so their plan went ahead. They knew that if the council staff opened and read that letter, they would be stopped instantly with an injunction.

No worries though, everything went to plan.

The caravans all started to move in on Saturday morning. A big tape measure was on hand to ensure that they split the long rectangular piece of land equally between the three.

Starting from the lane, the men had it worked out evenly. Paddy had already said that he would have the first section, so that he was next to the road, Michael had said that he wanted to be at the end so that everyone coming in or out would not keep passing his door. John Joe said, 'Look, guys, I am just happy to be on my own ground, I don't care where I go.' They had booked a local contractor with a JCB machine for nine o'clock on the Saturday morning. Also ordered were lorryloads of hard core to arrive hourly until the quarry closed; after this there would be no more until the next week, and by then the council would stop all works.

They had to complete this plan of moving in quickly, because they knew that once the council offices opened on Tuesday and the staff read the proposals submitted on the Friday, they would be down to see what the heck was going on at the piece of land. So speed was of the essence. The top layer of grass was scraped off before spreading the hard core bases, they then piled up the grass and earth to the far left and made a similar bank at the opposite end. After they had measured fairly between these two, they then erected two fences, evenly spaced, thus creating three plots for themselves and their families. All day Saturday the machine dug up the ground, moving muck and spreading stone. A team of Polish lads was brought in to mix all the concrete, dig the post holes and put up the fencing. There was plenty of sweat and hard work. Families' earnings, all of their savings, were being ploughed into this project, and all on a big chance. The travelling life was being squeezed out of existence, so these were tough measures.

The women had never made so many cups of tea or sandwiches. No-one could stop from this very important work. With the clock ticking, the men worked till very late. Sunday came, the work continued from Saturday, and Monday was just the same.

From the lane, you turned to your right and passed each plot on your left hand side. The first plot had a bank and a fence for its boundary, the second had two fences, and the third had a fence and a bank. With mature trees growing down both sides of this ground, this provided good screening from the open fields, and you didn't really notice the motorway at the end, so it really looked a nice environment for all involved. After a very hectic weekend the men had stood proudly on that Monday evening with their families, viewing the result of their hard work. Everyone was happy.

Tuesday morning arrived and, after feeling so anxious for the past few days, everyone was glad the hard work was finished and the place looked smart enough for anyone. Of course if they were allowed, they would improve things even more. They knew the council policy of not providing sites for travellers, it was always cutbacks or red tape. This drastic action which they had now taken was not what they wanted to do, but they felt they had no choice. They would have preferred to move from place to place on the open road, but that way of life had been taken away from them.

As nine o'clock came and went, then ten, then eleven, the fear of council reprisals seemed to evaporate and was replaced with joy. But in the end it had to happen, the dreaded visit. The families were expecting Gestapo-type men to turn up in force and heavy-handed, but that's not what happened. Two men in suits arrived just after three o'clock in the afternoon. They gave their names and told the occupiers that they had read the forms that had been submitted for planning permission to the council, that there was a slight error in one of the forms, and that they would call back in a couple of days. If help was needed to fill out the mistakes, they said they would show them how. They also, very helpfully, told the travellers that if they employed the services of a planning agent, it would help their case a lot. It was actually quite good of these council guys to take this approach.

The council was now appearing to be a little sympathetic to the travellers. This site was in nobody's way and it met most of the basic requirements. It was even lit up at night. Even though there was no electricity on site, the light from the lamp posts in the lane shone into the ground. With a relaxed frame of mind the men thought about approaching the farmer who owned the land at the rear of their property to see if it was possible to get the mains water connected through him. They would offer to pay him for this privilege. The following day the first visit to the farm seemed quite positive. The farmer was not there at the time, but his wife was very polite to them and did not seem to have any problems with her new neighbours.

A few weeks went by very quickly. The men went off to work every day, the children had been booked into the local school and there was even a doctor's surgery not far away if anyone got sick. So the families were all now feeling very happy with their hassle-free life on their own property; life was now looking good. Councils normally do not allow any further works to continue on a site if there are any court appearances involved, but these councillors did allow certain important items on the site including portaloos and gates to be erected, which was very fair of them.

The weeks slowly turned to months. One Sunday morning just after the families had been to mass, they all stood outside chatting away about nothing in particular. Out of the blue John Joe said, 'Where's Michael gone?' 'He was here a moment ago,' someone answered. 'Well, lads, I have been thinking,' John Joe continued. 'I thought when we came here that we split up this land into three equal plots.' 'Yes, you're right, we did. Why?' 'Well,' said John Joe, 'how come Michael's plot now looks bigger than ours.' They all looked across at Michael's pitch and sure enough it did look much bigger. 'When we see him, we will ask him about this, but maybe it's an illusion,' said one. With that the conversation changed, and strangely never got mentioned again.

Autumn came. Soon the leaves started to fall off the trees and it was raining more often, not heavy rain, but consistently, day in and day out. One afternoon while the men were out working and most of the women shopping, a group of people in red and yellow shiny jackets came walking over the motorway embankment and started to descend onto the caravan site. The youngsters at home were a little afraid of these men. 'What do you want?' they yelled out of the caravan windows, hoping their shouting would make the people go away. As the men approached they called out and apologised to the children, but they said it was very important that they should inspect the land by the motorway. They gave one of the older children one of their business cards. They were in fact the chief planners for the M25 motorway.

'We want to inspect the area urgently, because for a few weeks now this area of the motorway has come under a lot of stress,' the man explained. It was less than four years since the last major improvements had been done to the motorway there, but it was now showing large cracks and ageing yet should have taken at least twenty years to get that bad. It was fast becoming very dangerous for traffic. So they politely asked permission to walk along and inspect the banking in front of the motorway. They didn't really need to ask, they were just being respectful. Horrified, they soon discovered the reason for the near collapse of this side of the motorway. Michael had dug away a large area of the retaining banking which held up the motorway above, to make his plot a few yards wider. This, in fact, was what the men had noticed a few weeks back when it was noticed that Michael's plot was now larger.

With the heavy rains continuing for several weeks, the cracks in the motorway had become very deep and wide, meaning the motorway would have to be closed on this side. Lane closures for at least two months, all dug out, re-based and tarmaced would run up a bill of at least two million pounds for someone to pay. When the men came home and found out these massive problems, they decided to phone the council the next day to hear the truth from them. They were told, 'Yes, everything is true. We are about to instigate proceedings against you all for criminal damage and to seek massive compensation through the courts.' The men held a meeting immediately. First, they were bloody angry at Michael for what he had done, but they knew now the game was up. A decision was made straight away for everyone's future. That night all the trailers were hooked up and straight away they all drove to the motorway and – yes, you are right – as far away from this terrible problem as possible, before they all ended up in court, and possibly prison.

The Hurricane
and the Haystack

We had heard of the commotion down south. Men were having a laugh down the phone saying, 'Michael, I will come and tarmac for you for a lot less than two million quid.'

Unusually for us there had been no over-indulgence of alcohol the night before, so this bright and fresh morning was very welcome and had all the signs of being a good day to go out and hawk off a load of tarmac. Wigan Joe and myself jumped into the truck and headed off to the tarmac suppliers, Mather and Ellis, in Trafford Park and in no time entered the yard. What a little corner of the world this had become, almost exclusively for travellers. It had fresh materials delivered daily, unemployed workers stood at the gates looking for 'the shift' – a day's work – and, most importantly, when Peter the boss got to know your face you could load up and pay later. This was extremely handy when funds were low. It was very well located in the town, because if it wasn't for this yard you would have to trek some forty-five miles to Buxton in Derbyshire daily for your load. With Mather and Ellis you could turn up any time you fancied and, depending on your humour, could put as much or as little tarmac on your truck and go get a day's wage. With the cafe at the front for a chat with other travellers and to catch up on any gossip over a bite to eat, things could not have been better organised. This set-up lasted many years and nobody ever expected it to end, but like all good things eventually it did.

We called over for two labourers to join us. One was Michael the Priest, who got his name because it was said he had put his name down to train as a priest then failed the exams, and the other one was Jimmy O'Gorman; two fine Irish labourers. We motioned them to follow us into the yard, which they did. They knew exactly what to do next without so much as a word being spoken.

The pair of them vaulted up onto the back of the truck and rolled up the tarmac sheet, which was a heavy tarpaulin cover that we used to cover up the materials once we were loaded to keep them hot until we arrived at the job. They would then sit on top of it until we arrived at the job. These men knew exactly what we were doing. From experience they knew when we had jobs to go to, or when we were going out on the knocker looking for work. Some men did not want to work with you if you didn't have work booked in, because they knew that if you were on the knocker and got no jobs, then they would get no money either. That was the way it was in those days. But Jimmy and Michael had no such problems with us, they knew we always sold our load. If we were in tip-top form, we would put between five and eight tons on the truck. If the day felt slow, then we would put three to five tons on. Today we put five tons on. The logic was to stay local, and if you sold up quick, you could always nip back for some more tarmac, which we often did.

So, let's get on with the story. Wigan Joe and me, with the two men huddled on the back of the truck and five tons of Mather and Ellis hot tarmac and no real plans of where to go, decided to take a route down the main A6 road, leaving Manchester and heading down past the McVitie's biscuit factory. The sweet smell from the newly-baked biscuits floats in the air at certain times of the day and fairly makes your mouth water every time you drive. Turning right and then left on an instinctive whim, we found ourselves in a street where there was what we call 'chancy houses', ones that we think will be good for our business of tarmac. We got out of the truck, told the two men to wait for a while as we were going on the knocker, offering to resurface any drives or paths that we came across which needed doing.

Within ten minutes I was back at the truck with a big smile on my face. I had just agreed to do a nice big driveway resurface. I asked the men to bring their shovels and to start to take off the weeds on the driveway that I had just booked in. This was really all the preparation most jobs received from us. I drew the truck up to the front of the house and we started to fill up the wheelbarrows with the black gold, which is the name that we give to tarmac. This property was a large imposing Victorian-style house, with a large detached double garage, and you could easily imagine horses and carriages had been around here at some time in the past. It didn't take Wigan Joe long to notice that our truck had been moved from its previous place, which always indicated that there was a job on. 'Did you get one?' I casually asked Joe. 'Yes, a front path,' he said. 'And if the bloke likes what he sees, then he will give us the back to do as well.' We were very good at our job, and in those days we could lay the black gold very fast. As this decent-sized job was nearly finished, we found that over half our load was gone.

'I think we should slow down a bit, lads. You know what people are like if we finish too quickly.' This we did and, as we got nearly to the end of the job, I knocked on the door and asked the man indoors to come outside and take a look at what we had done for him. 'How do you like that then, mate?' I asked. He seemed generally satisfied with what we had achieved. As the small talk was going on, I noticed that his large garage was leaning badly through age, and needed serious work to rebuild it. So I just asked him if he fancied having it demolished. He told me no way, that his plans were to put a couple of snooker tables into it. At the time I had started to visit snooker halls to pass the odd hour. Realising that these things are massive places which charge a couple of pounds per hour with maybe thirty or forty tables, I said straight out, 'You won't make much of a living with snooker, mate.' 'Are you trying to be funny with me?' he said, with a look in his eyes that meant he did not like my remark. 'No,' I replied. 'Where's the harm in that?' 'Do you know who I am?' he asked. Wigan Joe had been listening to this and butted in, 'Here, lad, give me the money for the job and I'll be off then.' This man was gobsmacked as he handed out the money from his trouser pocket. 'I don't believe this,' he was saying at our general ignorance.

'What's the problem, pal?' I asked, now that the money was safely in our pocket and not his. 'I play snooker,' he said, 'and I earn a good living.' 'Who are you then?' we asked. 'Alex,' he said, 'Alex Hurricane Higgins. I am the present world champion.' We all looked at each other in silence. Alex thought we were going to ask for autographs, etc, but we didn't. Michael the Priest just asked him if he had a light for his roll-up.

Wigan shouted, 'Come on, you lot, I have work to do.' And he dragged us all across the street to the next job.

The man across the street decided not to have the back of his property laid with tarmac, just the front. So we finished the small path, put up the tools and drove for a few miles to some different houses and started again. It shouldn't take long now to get rid of the last of the load, we thought. And it didn't. We had driven back in towards town, gone past Man United's football ground and ended up in Broughton, next to The Cliff, United's training ground. We knew that these houses were usually okay for our trade. We had worked there before, so the streets were known to us. Confident that we would finish off the load, we again got knocking; this was our way of life. In no time Joe had got a job and the way things looked it would take everything we had on the back of the truck. 'This woman wants this job doing as a birthday surprise to her husband,' Joe told us. 'He will be home shortly, so if we can finish quickly and be gone before he arrives, she will be happy.' We too hoped we would be finished before he arrived home, as what we had done would be a surprise for him – but maybe not a nice one, if you know what I mean. Being the man on the rake whose job it was to level the tarmac, I had gone to the shop for a packet of cigs. Wigan Joe had just been told to get the job finished quick and had handed the rake to a worker, who pleaded with him that he was not good at levelling up. But he was just told by Joe to get on with it, which he did. By the time that I got back, the job was in a shocking state. As the last bit of tarmac went down, the lady was paying up. The men were told to get a move on because somebody would have something to say about this lot; the job would last but, by God, it was ugly. Me and Joe walked to the front of the truck and started to split up the money that had been collected that day. As we stood there chatting, a taxi pulled up outside the house we had been working on, and this great fucking giant of a man mountain unrolled himself out of the car. He was enormous, 24 stone. 'Fuck me!' I said. 'I hope that's not her husband, if it is we are in the shit here.' I knew the job was sub-standard, but of course she was happy with it.

Sure enough, into the front gate he went, then he saw the workmen, and next thing there were raised voices. Joe said to me, 'Did you recognise that big guy?' 'Yes,' I said. 'He seems familiar but I can't place him.' 'Well, you watch wrestling sometimes, don't you?' 'Of course, it's Giant Haystacks, the professional wrestler. Quick! For fuck's sake, get the men and the few tools onto the truck.' He had gone into the house and we could hear shouting coming from the inside. He was pretty angry with his wife.

'Joe!' I shouted. 'Get the men and tools now, I will start the truck up.' The men came running out with rakes and shovels and threw them onto the truck, then Joe jumped in the front, the other two in the back of the truck. 'If they fall off, keep going,' said Joe, thinking of his own skin. I was panicking and laughing at this, as he said, 'Well, if he falls, I am not going back to pay him. He can fuck off.' I was in stitches laughing at this. In my haste to get the fuck out of there quickly, I stalled the engine. Next thing we heard really loud shouting and bad language, it was Haystacks running out of the front door like a big steam locomotive, shaking his fists and cursing, 'I want to see you bastards!' Just then the engine fired up, I put it into first, lots of revs, and we were slowly pulling away from this house. He managed to get two hands on the back of the truck and I am sure that he was going to lift it up to stop us pulling away. But I hit the brakes hard and he banged into the rear of the truck and let go. In that instant I let the clutch out again and we shot forward and away. We pulled into a pub car park about three miles down the road, because we all needed a drink. We were all making our excuses if we got caught. Joe was pleading his innocence, he never levelled the job; I was laughing like mad, I never did anything; the men were trembling. We all were.

The men told us that he had been yelling at them, 'I will get you bastards, mark my words!' They shit themselves on the back of that truck. 'Boss, his face kept staring at us. He was fuming,' they said. We stayed put for an hour and had a few pints, then with Dutch courage we ventured outside to the truck, confident that there were four of us. I knew that if he was there I was just going to run like fuck. All was well, he wasn't to be seen, so we fucked off home very smartly. Not bad money for a day's pay, but boy did we earn it. It was a close call, but we got away and lived to lay tarmac for another day. Those two men wouldn't come to work with us for ages after that, they told everybody that we were mad. Me and Joe separated for a while, if either one of us got captured we could blame the other.

The Brick in the Wheel

Wigan Joe and Ned Collins were driving from Manchester to Buxton in Derbyshire early one morning. They were going to get a load of tarmac for a job that they had on in Manchester. This journey was a job in itself – the old type trucks, the mountainous roads, the heavy haul back. The bigger the load, the greater the stress, but the more you would earn.

It was very early, five-thirty in fact, on a cold winter's morning, in a truck with no heater. Just normal stuff to these men with this way of life; there was no room for any petting here. An early start was important. First, it was a long way to go to get tarmac, secondly, they had to get back in good time to lay the hot tarmac at the place where their men would be waiting to complete the job. Also, if you got to the quarry before six o'clock, there was a good chance you could get the tarmac very cheap as the men who started work early were always on the fiddle. The manager always arrived after 6am, which gave the men who worked there the chance to sell cheap, put the money in their pockets and claim wastage for any discrepancy that may occur.

As Joe and Ned drove, they suddenly saw in the rear view mirror lights being flashed at them. Thinking it was the police, they pulled over but to their relief it wasn't. It was a motorist telling them that they had a brick lodged between the double back wheels at the back of the truck. They thanked him and went to look at the problem. Sure enough, there was a large brick jammed between the rear tyres. They realised this could be dangerous for any vehicle travelling behind them. If the brick came loose, it could fly into the air and maybe go through someone's windscreen. They stood looking at this problem for a short while and then decided that one of them would have to lay down on his back and knock this brick out somehow.

Danny, being the younger and fitter, volunteered to do the job. 'Pass me an iron bar, Joe,' Danny told him. But after twenty minutes of trying to knock out the brick, the job was proving to be more difficult than they first thought. There was a very chilly wind and now with both hands frozen, the job had become even harder. The brick was still firmly lodged. Because of where they had stopped, the road had become restricted to one lane with traffic now getting backed up behind them. About ten vehicles back in the queue, an angry truck driver got out of his vehicle and walked purposely up to the stranded truck. He was a very big chap and strode up to Wigan Joe and demanded that they move this heap of shit straight away. He knew that it would take more than a neck warmer to get away from this one.

'Don't go on at me, mate,' Wigan Joe told him, very wary of this huge man. 'Tell him!' And he pointed to Danny lying on his back under the truck. The angry driver looked the truck up and down. 'As usual, no bloody tax on it,' he said. The wheelbarrows, rakes and tarmac tools in the back, and the towbar told the story, bloody gypsies. 'Hey, tinker!' he said, shouting at Danny. 'Move this fucking heap of shit out of my way, before

I move it.' Danny looked up, 'I will, sir. As it happens, I have just finished this little job I had to do.' And he slid out from under the lorry and the awkward position he had been lying in. He stood up and looked at this giant of a man and asked, 'Why have you been abusive, using bad language this early in the morning?' Ned, who had a very short temper and was afraid of no man, did not wait for the answer. He punched the driver hard in the ribs several times in very quick succession. The man crumpled to the ground in severe pain. 'Come on, Joe,' Ned said. 'Let's get out of here.' And he got into the truck.

'What a cheeky, mouthy bastard he was,' he complained as he started the engine and pulled away. Wigan Joe shouted, 'I knew what you would do when you got up, that's why I said nothing.'

'I like to hit the big ones,' Ned replied laughing, 'they always go down with a bang.' They continued on their way, still laughing at what had happened so early in the morning, but got to the quarry too late for the cheap tarmac. 'Well, Ned,' Joe said, 'you got some satisfaction out of knocking that big bastard down, but now we have to pay the full price for the tarmac. We can't win!'

What a Week!

Tommy Moran was a large man who always wore a trilby. He could be heard from afar with his loud deep Irish brogue. Always the one to have a deal or to help make a deal, he was legendary, and very good at his job.

If he got into a temper, and he often did, he would raise his already fearsome voice and boom out at whoever. Arms waving, fists curled into a ball, plenty of animation, that was Tommy. Maybe in his day he just let fly with his fists; I did hear that he had been a handful years back. These days though, you could weather the storm and just stand well back if you were the unlucky recipient of his wrath. He would crook you in a moment if you let your guard down, anyone who fell for his Irish blarney was in for being relieved of some cash. He would openly tell people his tales of kissing the Blarney Stone and would then sell them a small fancy coloured pebble. For good luck, he would say. No matter what money he earned that day, little or much, Tommy always had his head switched on. He would not let a punter pass him by. He was the envy of some men because there were times that he could sit in a pub drinking all day and it would not cost him a penny.

On this busy Saturday afternoon in the pub, just down from where the caravans were stationed on a large town centre car park, Tommy was telling all who would listen about how he had started to tarmac a job for a farmer, and had got a sub off him halfway through the work in order to go and buy more materials. Later the same day he had received a phone call to say that somebody who was a close friend had died and was getting buried in Ireland the next day. So with no spare time to tell the farmer what was going on, he had gone to the funeral, spent some time with the deceased man's family, attended at the graveside then promptly returned back home, some two-and-a-half days later. In the meantime the farmer had got it into his head that the tarmac area to be finished off was far greater than the area promised by Tommy. Once Tommy returned the two men had spoken at length but to no avail; the pair were deadlocked over the situation. The farmer was now wishing that he had never met Tommy, and he was getting annoyed with the whole situation.

Tommy had taken half of the money and spent it, and the job was now a lot bigger than was priced for, so there really was no profit left in finishing it off, or if indeed it covered the costs. All of the tools and the machine roller that Tommy had left in the farmer's yard were now a bargaining chip for the farmer. 'You don't get your stuff back,' he had said, 'until you agree to finish off all the work.'

My father had been listening to all of this story and said, 'Tommy, just go back and take your things, they are yours.' 'That's right,' said Tommy, 'but the farmer said he would call the police and take the vehicle number if the tools were removed.'

Tommy was getting into more of a state with every pint, reliving his terrible plight. He always kept good machines for his work, and now he stood to lose one, through what he felt was no fault of his own.

70

'I would give very good money to have my stuff back,' declared Tommy to the listening group, and he said just how much he would give. Eyebrows raised at this offer. My father asked him to repeat this again, which Tommy did, followed by, 'When that machine is parked outside my caravan door, I will pay up. The smaller tools I am not so worried about.

'I know that you are good,' Tommy said to my father, 'but this is an impossible situation I am in.' My father never answered, but just ordered more of his favourite Martel brandy and carried on drinking it, along with his bottle of Guinness as a chaser. The afternoon carried on with witty banter between the travelling men as usual, but during this time my father had quietly left the pub unnoticed. Within the hour my father was back and all heads turned as he noisily entered the bar.

'Tommy,' he announced. 'Go outside and pay that taxi, then walk the short distance to your caravan and take a look.' Tommy was half-tipsy by now but curiosity made him do what he had been told. Ten minutes later Tommy returned. The short walk and the sight that greeted him had put him back on top form. 'Alec, you wizard, how the hell did you do it?' Before Tommy got his answer, my father told him to forget the money that he had promised and just get everyone a beer each to celebrate. 'For God's sake, tell us!' By now everybody wanted to know. 'How did you get that roller back here?'

My father told him, 'Very simple, lads. The most difficult problem usually has an easy answer. I telephoned a taxi while you were all drinking, and asked for a younger driver rather than an elderly one, and a car with a tow bar. I offered the cab firm a little extra, telling them I needed to collect something. They readily agreed to this. We went to the farm and I told the young man to hop out and hook up the roller and trolley, which he did. As we were leaving the yard, the farmer asked me what I was doing. I told him that I owned the roller now and that if he had any problems they were nothing to do with me. The farmer just stood there stumped, and looked on as we drove off.'

The whole pub erupted into laughter. 'Alec, they all say that you are good, well I know now, first hand, that you really are.' The men laughed and drank into the night.

"Black Alec", Mr Thompson to his customers, could talk the birds down from the trees

The Next Day

Tommy Moran had a visitor at his door. It was seven-thirty in the morning, but no matter what passed Tommy's lips the night before, be it whisky or brandy and port along with the pints of beer, he would wake and be out of bed in no time. He recognised the voice calling his name. It was his long time friend, Joe Grundy. As Joe entered the caravan the shine off the fine bone china plates and cut glass vases illuminated everywhere. 'Bit bright in here, Tommy,' Joe said. 'It's the way Bridgey likes it,' came back the reply. 'You two better not go off drinking today,' called a tired head from under the quilt. Bridget knew only too well what to expect when these two got together. 'No,' said Joe, 'I am here to see if Tommy wants to go hawk off a bit of tarmac today, that's all. Now that he has his roller back!' he said in mock sarcasm. Once Bridgey heard this, she settled back into her rest.

The two men chatted over a cup of tea, made their plans and jumped into the truck parked outside. Wigan Joe had heard all about the story from the previous day and as they drove to pick up labourers, they had a laugh going over the details once again. Joe and Tommy drove to the workers and nodded at two men to join them. Manchester and Michael the Priest.

Manchester, whose name was Tony, had insisted on having a nickname like most of the other men.

He figured that being a fairly newcomer, yet always drinking, working and mixing with the Irish lads, it was only right that he had a name put on him. He kept on about it so much that one day we asked him where he was from, and out it came, Manchester. So it stuck for years. As long as we knew him, the only name we ever called him was Manchester; he hated it. Served him right really, he wanted something exotic like 'Too True', or the Priest or Corky. These real men were only ever known like this because nobody cared about what anybody's name was. The workers were every bit as much characters as the travellers were. I think it rubbed on to all of us, the craic.

Now, back to the story.

Having got Manchester, Michael the Priest and a load of tarmac, they all set off from Trafford Park in the direction of Altrincham and towards the posh houses. 'Pull in, Tommy, and get diesel,' Wigan Joe said. So at the next garage they swung into the forecourt and cheated a big Mercedes car to the next available petrol pump. The men didn't listen to the little fat Scotsman doing his nut, but some lads walking past did. The short legs on this man barely kept his long overcoat off the ground. His cigar was flapping wildly, he was fuming, but nobody took any notice. Joe and Tommy bought their cigs and paid for the diesel, then started to get back in the truck. The young lads walking past started to descend on our two and became aggressive. Joe and Tommy wasted no time. 'Get in, Manchester!' they shouted at the worker for taking his time on the way back from the toilet. The truck sped off with all on board, leaving a trail of people intent on having a bust-up. It was quiet in the cab for a moment, then Manchester said, 'Did you get his autograph?' 'Who?' the men asked. 'Matt Busby, the bloke in the Merc, the one you pushed in front of.' 'Did we fuck!' Joe said very annoyed. 'Who the fuck is he?' They had never heard of this man, the manager of the glorious Manchester United.

Manchester, the worker, explained in the only way he knew how. 'You know how I work for you, boss,' he said. 'Well that big football ground at the back of us is Old Trafford, and the fat bloke is the boss of all them fellers that kicks the ball around.' The lads were obviously fans walking past who had seen everything and didn't like it.

The men couldn't believe it. 'That cunt nearly got us beaten up!'

Our two could not see that they had caused everything.

It was soon forgotten a few miles down the road as the men started to knock on a few doors, looking for their livelihood. Tommy got a job and Wigan Joe, leaving them to it, went looking for the next one. Feeling peckish, Joe walked into a butcher's shop for a couple of slices of roast ham to nibble on to keep the hunger away until they had chance to find a decent cafe and get some breakfast, even though by now it was nearer dinner time. As Joe got served, he told the man behind the counter that he had a load of material left over off a big contract and could the butcher make any use of it? 'Sure, just what I need to tidy up the back of my premises,' he said. So Joe walked out the back and, after a quick measure up, gave a fair price for the work and the deal was made. With a firm handshake Wigan Joe said that he would do it straight away. Quickly as possible they all set about finishing the first job and moving onto the next.

As the rear yard was underway, the butcher came out and said, 'You won't forget to shift that big lump of timber, will you, lads? It is in with the deal as we agreed.' 'Yes,' Joe nodded. The very long railway sleeper was to go as agreed. He had been hoping to leave it, but now he knew that this lump would have to be shifted. The workers laid their tarmac over the yard and were intending to leave it behind as well, but they agreed, 'We had better shift it, in case we don't get paid.'

This big, heavy, long and very slippery railway sleeper, which was patchy green with damp and growth on it, was a real handful. Bending down, lifting it knee high, they all started to head for the back gate. Inching forward all four of them made progress, but as they reached the gate, this big object had to be lifted higher to get it out and around the narrow gateway. The men got a couple of lads who were walking past to help them. Just as the thing was inching out and job done, it needed one last heave to finish. 'Push, Michael! Push, Manchester!' they said... and it was out.

'Take it a couple of yards down out of the way,' Joe said. They did, but just as they were all feeling good, somebody let slip with their grip. Shit! The fucking big lump fell straight onto the front of the butcher's brand new delivery van. Right on the corner it fell. The bonnet, the radiator, the bumper and the headlight broke like a biscuit. 'We are bollocksed, what can we do?' They stood and looked at each other. The helpers fled. 'Sorry, mate, it's not our fault,' they muttered as they left pronto. 'Manchester, you fucking jackass! Take off your jackets, all of you!' Joe ordered the men. 'What?' the men said. 'You heard me, take off your jackets, and your jumpers too.' The men followed orders, then Joe collected the clothes together and placed them all over the damaged area of the van. 'Now, men,' he said. 'When I bring the butcher here to look at the finished work, I will also be getting paid, so you must wipe the sweat from your brow, even though it's cold, and pretend that you do not need the top layers on. Just play act until I get the old Guinness vouchers, OK lads?' The workers began to sweep up and stand around the van to hide what had happened, whilst Wigan Joe got his money.

The plan worked, the butcher was guided past his van, told to inspect the work, and Joe congratulated the men on such a fine finish. 'Can you pay me, boss?' he said. 'I really have to go quickly.' He wasn't lying. He needed to go before the mess was discovered. They shot off home, paid the workers, and called it a day.

Face to Face
With the Hangman

A couple of days had passed since the butcher's van episode, and our two amigos were well rested and ready to go out looking for a living once more. 'Where shall we head for?' they asked each other. 'Well, away from any fucking football grounds!' Tommy laughingly said. 'Yes, and no more butcher's for a while either,' said Joe Grundy. They both smiled at the thought.

Once again it was down to the tarmac yard where they enlisted the services Michael the Priest and Jimmy O'Gorman, along with a bigger than average load of tarmac. These boys were raring to go. As they drove they chatted. 'Did you hear what happened last week?' Tommy said to Joe. 'Well, the story goes that some men were tarmacing a driveway and the lady of the house happened to remark at how dark it was at the front of her house during the night time. These men, spotting the chance to have a laugh, said to the woman, "Well you should have these new white chippings installed into your driveway, missus. They glow in the dark, they illuminate, they are fluorescent." They were shuddering with laughter, then suddenly the lady's face lit up and she declared that they must put these wonderful things into her pathway. The men got afraid at this silly lie, and told her that there was none left, but no, she insisted that she would pay whatever it cost to have them. With this, the pound signs were in the men's eyes.' 'What happened then?' asked Joe, all interested in this story. 'Well the men pretended to drive off and get the illuminating chippings for her. They returned half an hour later with a bag of normal white spar chippings and told her that these were "the special ones" and she agreed to pay extra for this luxury. Just as the men started to scatter them into the tarmac and put the roller over them to press them into the surface, the woman's husband turned up. Unknown to the rest of them, once the husband had heard this tale from his wife he walked indoors and within minutes came back outside again. ''These chippings don't glow,'' he declared. ''How's that then?'' the men asked him. ''Because I took some indoors into the bedroom and closed the curtains, and trust me, they don't glow or shine at all.'' The men, shocked and full of disbelief, were quick. ''No, mister, it has to be natural dark, not forced.'' He fell for it, but I heard that what started out as a laugh got serious, and the men left town, afraid of getting arrested. They have not been seen around again for a long time.'

'He must have been a posh nutter,' Michael the Priest said. 'If he had just put some into his jacket pocket and looked down into it, he would see if they did shine or not.' 'Be quiet, Michael, you jackass, you fucking idiot,' they all said together. 'Enough of this, let's get some hawking done.' Michael looked all dazed, he didn't know what he had done wrong.

'Pull into the garage, Tommy. Let's get dieseled up,' said Wigan Joe. An old trick of the trade was to pour a drop of diesel over the load to make it more pliable if it was getting too sticky. As they approached the pumps, Joe said, 'Michael, you get up on the back of the truck and squirt diesel on the load and put some in the tank. I will go and pay for it.' So off they went. Whilst queueing up at the counter, Joe heard an almighty whoosh. Michael the Priest had done as he was told alright, he had stood on the top of the tarmac with the pump in his hand, had squirted the hand-held pipe down onto the load... the petrol pump. With the lighted cigarette in his mouth, you know the rest.

The blast threw him over the side of the truck and he fell on his ear. Luckily he let go of the pump in his hand and thus stopped the flow of petrol. But what a fright! His eyelids were singed, the tip of his nose and his chin were burned. He looked a right state. 'Michael, you thick bastard!' the men screamed.

There must have been somebody looking down on them that day, as things could have been a lot worse. Apart from the Priest being shook up, there was no real harm done. Again, as is becoming the norm, the men bolted for freedom. They decided to put plenty of distance between them and that garage, and didn't stop driving until they reached the outskirts of Ormskirk, near Southport.

'Michael, you fucking head case! Do you want to go home?' he was asked. 'No way,' he replied. The day's pay was more important. And so the men set to, to try and find work. Tommy got a job to tarmac, and then another.

There was no sign of Wigan Joe; he had been missing for ages. Concerned at this mystery, Tommy started out to look around and just as he did, Joe appeared. 'Where have you been?' he asked. 'With my new mate,' Joe said.

Puzzled, Tommy dug deeper, questioning his friend. 'Well,' said Joe, 'did you see that chap trimming his hedge earlier on down that lane?' 'Yes,' said Tommy. 'His name is Albert.' 'So?' 'So, he is the man that I have been speaking with for the last two hours. He is famous, sort of. He is the man who hangs everybody; men and women, the lot. His name is Albert Pierrepoint. He has been all over the world hanging, he hung twenty-five people in one day in Africa.' 'For fuck's sake, Joe!' said Tommy. 'He won't hang us, will he? Keep that bastard away from me,' he said in mock horror.

'Look at this book he has given to me. He signed it as well, look.' 'Fuck the book, Joe, go and look for more work. Let's sell this load and get off home.' And that's what they did. They went home and forgot all about the day's events, putting it all down to a day's work.

The Pine Doors
and the Boxer

With most jobs, and in life, there is repetition. Ours is the same but not all that often. What gets repeated with us is not what average people come to expect.

We never know when or how it will happen, even though we are creating the circumstances.

Tommy and Joe decided that enough had happened between them over the last few days so they split up for a while. I saw Wigan Joe in the pub and we spoke for a while. We agreed to call each other the next morning and go out together and look for some work. Swapping and changing partners was normal. Everything was for today only, unless you had made a plan with someone to stay together for a while.

We met up at seven o'clock the next morning at Mather and Ellis tarmac yard. The place never opened before eight, so this gave everybody who was there early the chance to have a chat and catch up on what had been happening lately. Many a false rumour had been started at these gates for a laugh. The place was closing down, the price of materials were about to double through the oil crisis, the police are looking for some body, etc, etc.

This was a fine morning, with clear skies. A great day for looking for work. Who should drive into the yard other than Tommy Moran, with a new partner. His big yellow truck was now a shiny blue. 'Better safe than sorry, eh?' he said to Joe, with a wink. A large can of paint and a brush in one of the worker's hands had done the trick. The idea was that all of yesterday's unintended mischief was down to a different coloured truck, and not today's colour. They knew that hopefully no vehicle numbers had been taken, so this should suffice. And it did, more and more often. Some trucks were painted so regularly that they would never rust. They also ran out of colours. Once the normal blue, red, yellow and green were used, things got tricky. Often when a man was looking to buy a truck off someone that he didn't trust, he would scratch it in a corner to see how many times it had been painted, and even ask what areas he should keep away from.

Mischief abounded during these times, it kept people on their toes, but the banter soon stops when the gates are opened for business. The first person in the queue of trucks is the first to be loaded and gone, off to an early start.

We headed out with our load as normal, the two workers were sitting quietly in the cab as we got out at some decent-looking houses and started to root out some work. A builder gave us the first job of the day, a long lane leading to a six bedroom detached older-type house. 'Tarmac the driveway, lads, and if you finish for dinner I will be back to pay you then,' he had said. He was also doing other work on the property, so he needed to go for materials. The driveway was on his list of jobs for the customer, so we would save him time which would let him do other things. We assured him that things would be finished for 12 o'clock, no problem. 'Be sure to take away all that stuff with you, junk, rubbish, the lot,' he had said as he left.

The job complete, the rubbish loaded, and with time to spare, we went a mile down the road to Stretford council tip by the side of the M602 motorway. We shovelled off the muck and rubbish that had been taken off the driveway and, as we did the machine driver in the yard, the man whose job it was to scrape the ground clean with his big giant tractor and keep everything heaped up, came across to us and offered to buy the ten doors off us that we were dumping. Okay, they had a bit of brass around the pine handles, old brass hinges even, but to us they had no value so we were very happy at this. He paid us a fiver a door and loaded them into a van, then his mate drove off with them. 'If you get any more,' he said, 'bring them here. We sell loads of them to a dealer.' Our workers by now had finished off loading the muck so we left feeling happy, and eagle-eyed looking for more of these doors.

Still in good time, we waited back at the house for our money from the builder. He arrived smiling, which is always a good sign, but then the smile dropped. 'Where are the doors?' he said. 'I have taken them off from the indoors so that I can shave a bit off the bottom of them, as I am laying all new fitted carpets in the house.' Our stomachs tightened, we had fucked up again. We had followed orders and moved all the rubbish, how were we supposed to know?

We told the builder that they were on the tip. 'Good,' he said, ' it's not far, we will go and retrieve them.' Horror! So with no choice, one of us told him that they saw the big JCB bulldoze them into a big heap and that they had been squashed and broken. The builder had been having a great day before he met us, but it couldn't be our fault, could it? We stayed quiet for a moment and the builder stood and thought. Fair play to him, he handed over our money to us and said, 'Here, lads, it's not your fault. I told you to take everything away.'

That was a close one, Joe and I agreed.

We drove off for a few miles and Wigan Joe said to me, 'Pull in at the next shops while I get a bottle of beer to settle my nerves. All of this excitement,' he said jokingly, 'is getting to me.' I said okay and, as I pulled across the road to ask a person walking by for directions to the nearest shops, I heard a sickening crunch, a slight thud and glass breaking. My heart started to thump heavily. What had I done? The speed was only twenty odd miles an hour, but I had obviously hit something. As I pulled over, a motorbike could be seen very close by the side of us; too close, on its side. 'That fucking idiot!' Joe yelled through the open window, loud enough for the rider to hear as he lay on the ground with this big heavy bike pinning him down. I jumped out and while I could see that the man was not hurt, I thought that I would get my word in first, following on from Joe. 'That was a bit daft,' I said to him, standing right over him. The wheels, slowly spinning, were coming to a halt, the bars were bent, the front headlight and number plate broken.

'Give him a tenner for his trouble and let's get going,' Joe called from his seat in the truck. 'You will not!' this bloke said as he got up. 'You will give me twenty.' I couldn't believe that this was happening. 'Yes, okay, I will give you twenty,' I blurted out. This was all happening so fast. As the man slid out from under his bike, he rose to well over six foot. He stood with his chest into my face, took the twenty pound note that I was holding out, and said, 'If I ever get you in there...' and he pointed in a straight line dead ahead to Stretford Police station, half a mile down the road. It was notorious for the tough treatment meted out. As he said this, I caught sight of the bold faded imprint in his leathers, POLICE. Shaking inside, I knew what he meant. With perfect timing, Wigan Joe called out, 'Let's get going, son.' Relief? I don't know what it's called, but I did the same as everybody else at a sticky time, I fucked off home.

The beer got drunk that night with slightly shaky hands.

And yes, true to form, the yellow truck was green by the next day.

The following morning was greeted with a lot of caution. 'He never asked to see your licence or insurance,' Wigan Joe said to me, trying to reassure me. 'That's true,' I thought, 'but then again he was dazed and off duty. It all happened so fast.' His mates would have plenty to say though if they come across me, this I knew for certain. 'Oh, fuck it, just keep going with the head down,' said Joe. 'He is right,' I thought, and this cheered me up. The old saying came filtering through, 'If you worry, you will die. If you don't worry, you still die. So, what's the point?' Just keep out of Stretford for a while, I told myself.

'Where shall we go working then?' I said. 'Cheetham Hill,' said Joe. 'That's not a good area for us really,' I replied. 'Ah,' said Joe, 'I have had my eye on a few factories behind the prison for a while now, and a new owner has told me to call back in and see him about some work.' 'They'll put you in there one day,' I said.

'They already did that. I got three months for pinching scrap metal,' Joe said and we fell about laughing.

So that was it, we headed off to Strangeways and the factories that stood at the rear. We found the call back, the boss was pleasant and, after a few minutes negotiating, we had the job booked in. It was a large parking area to level, hard core, and tarmac, so we told the boss that with today being Saturday we would make a fresh start on Monday morning. He happily agreed with this, but we had other plans. We knew just by looking that, being an open area, the car park was freely accessible all weekend. So if we prepared the job by hand on Sunday with extra labourers and plenty of hard core, while nobody was at work looking at us, we could in fact tell the boss that we had used a JCB at six in the morning on the Monday before he had arrived for work. This would mean Brownie points for us for being up so early and working so efficiently. The cheap labour would save us from renting a digger and driver. It sounded good, so that was that until the next day.

The following morning at half past seven it was gloomy and misty. Cheetam Hill Road is not the most welcoming of places on a quiet Sunday, with deserted factories and being in a red light district. At a quarter-to-eight in the morning, bad after the beer, hair tossed and uncombed, and hugging a parka jacket with a broken zip around me, I was trying to keep warm by standing shuffling my feet. I was stranded. There was no point sitting in the truck, it had no heater. It was fully loaded with hard core that could not be tipped off, so I could not drive off for a while. A fag hung lazily on one side of my mouth, while the men were digging like mad to keep warm. With no traffic around, the place looked like a ghost town and the lone figure standing in the doorway seemed surreal. Wearing a party dress, not wanting to give in, this lady of the night must have needed one more customer.

There were cafes but none would be open today for a warm cup of coffee. As I took in these surroundings, my mind wandering aimlessly, wondering what time any local pub would open its doors. I saw a figure running towards me; a long way off, but running. He got nearer and nearer as I enjoyed this simple distraction. I had no idea where Joe had got to, he was probably rooting round for scrap in and out of the yards. What appeared to be a young man was now very close by, he was breathing hard, with warm steam bellowing from his wide nostrils. My mind raced. What had he been doing? Who was he running from? Why is he not in bed? 'Probably pinched a few car radios,' I thought.

'What the fuck's going on here then?' I said. He had a hood on and didn't hear me properly. 'What's happening?' I asked as he drew to a halt, pausing for breath. I looked at this face in front of me. 'Chris,' I said, 'what brings you here?' Blimey, it was Chris Eubank training for his big clash with Nigel Benn at Old Trafford later that week. 'Fuckin' hell,' I thought, 'good job he didn't know what I was just thinking.'

'How's the fight gonna go?' I asked him, looking for a tip. 'Just watch,' he said, 'just you watch.' And he was gone. 'Joe,' I called, 'Joe. Let's go.' I told him of the last few minutes. Imagine if I had got lippy with Chris Eubank? I slapped it on thick. 'I was gonna give him a crack, one of your neck warmers.' Joe looked over as only a loving parent can, with a soft smile. 'Imagine if he had heard me,' I thought. This has been some week-and-a-half for all of us.

Monday we can all start afresh. What a week it's been. What a week!

And we did just that, finished up what we had to do and then I skipped town for a while. As I always do for the least thing. Keep things fresh, don't allow things to get stale.

Farewell, My Dear Friend

I had been travelling around Scotland for a few months looking for work, and I now decided to head back towards Manchester and go see my uncle and close friend, Joe Grundy, who lived off Regent Road in Salford. It was a busy Friday night when I arrived there. So, knowing how Joe loved to drink on a Friday night, I started to look for him in some of the local pubs. But after a while I gave up. I could find him nowhere, so I headed for his home and, sure enough, there he was lying down on the settee, half-asleep. 'Not out drinking, Joe?' I asked him, as we sipped a cup of tea and caught up on things. Looking at him sitting there, I felt very uneasy. He looked like he had lost a lot of weight, his face had no colour; he did not look very well at all. He told me that he had not been eating too well, so I advised him that tomorrow he should go and see a doctor. 'Nobody likes going in them places,' he said. But he assured me that he would go because things were not as they should be, and he knew it.

I stayed for another hour and he ended up asking me to leave because he was so tired. This was not the Joe Grundy that I had known and loved since I was a young boy. I decided to go and have a few beers to put my mind straight. By now I was very concerned for him. For this man not to be going out for a beer, especially on a Friday night, meant something was badly wrong here. The following day I had to go to the bank to cash a cheque in St Helen's, so I decided to call round to see Joe and ask him if he wanted to come with me for a drive and keep me company like old times. Although he was a little reluctant to do this, he eventually agreed, so long as we did not stay out too long. So at nine-thirty that morning we headed off down the East Lancs Road on our fifteen mile trip.

As we drove along we chatted and laughed as we reminisced about some of the old times we had been through. He seemed a lot better than when I had seen him the previous night. In no time at all we were at the bank and Joe waited in the car while I quickly slipped into the bank to get my money. Once I had the £280 in my hand from the bank teller, I went smartly back to the car where Joe was waiting. I asked him if he would like to join me on the knocker for a couple of hours and get some tarmac work booked in. 'I would love to,' was his reply, 'but to tell you the truth, I have hardly any energy to walk about right now. Maybe another day when I feel a bit better,' he said.

'Joe, it's okay, that's not a problem for me at all,' I told him. 'So, why don't I go and get us a sandwich? I am sure we are both hungry and could eat right now.' 'No, not for me,' he sighed. 'But Joe, you have always had a massive appetite, and you told me you had no breakfast this morning. So what's the problem? Come on, tell me.'

He told me that he seemed to always have a sore throat, and that it hurt him to eat anything solid. Sometimes when he tried hard to force food down, he would vomit. Now I was really concerned for him. Was it just a passing virus he had, or something much more serious? 'So how long have you had these problems, Joe?' I asked him. 'Oh, about a month now,' he told me. 'Go and get yourself a sandwich,' he said, 'don't worry about me.' As I had not had any breakfast either, I thought I must get at least a sandwich as I was feeling quite hungry by now. I nipped out to a baker's shop I had seen not far from the bank, ordered a sandwich for myself and noticed they did home-made hot soup to take away. Suddenly I had a good idea. 'Could you pass me a paper cup?' I asked the young girl who was serving me. 'And could I borrow your Sellotape for a minute?' I quickly explained to her what I was going to do and why. She smiled at me. 'That's a nice thing you are doing for your friend,' she told me laughing. I took a fifty pound note out of the money I had just received from the bank, folded it in half and wrapped it around the paper cup, then taped it on tightly. The girl then filled it with delicious home-made soup. 'Now, can you give me another empty cup and put lids on them both?' The other customers were now laughing at my antics. 'If he eats this soup without spilling any of it, he gets to keep the fifty pounds,' I told them. With plenty of smiles in the shop I paid the girl and left. As I approached the car, I put my sandwich in my pocket, wrapped my hands around each of the two identical cups, but I held the one with the money taped to it slightly higher in my grip, just so you could see a little of the note.

Standing at the car with Joe in the front seat, I said, 'I have some home-made soup here and it is very tasty. One is a surprise and one is a flop, you only get one chance so choose carefully.' We used to trick each other over the years, so this was just another of our little games. He picked carefully with a bit of eyes from me and won the right cup. 'Now,' I told him, 'this is a two-parter. You own the soup, and to get the money you must finish the contents with no spillage.' He perked up lovely, and with a big smile said, 'You're on.'

He did complain, 'It's bleedin' roasting,' but was never so happy.

We made our way back down the Lancs and sip by hot sip the cup went down. Our plans were made to get to the pub by half past ten just as the doors were opening. Things went quiet for a while, we were happy in each other's company driving along and we would get the craic going once we got to the pub. Then all of a sudden, 'For Fuck's sake!'

I thought Joe had flipped. 'I must be going crazy. The Curse of God!' he shouted out. 'What a stupid fucked-up thing I have done.' 'Joe, what's going on, what's the matter with you, why are you cursing so bad?' As I said this my eyes went down to his empty hands. He didn't need to speak, but the words fell out anyway. 'The soup was so nice that I totally forgot everything,' he said. 'The nifty, the lot, I chucked it out ages ago.' Sick as the thing that sits on Long John's shoulder, I knew that I would have to give him another fifty because it had been my dumb idea with the cup. He was also sick because he had been dreaming of having a few hours out. 'Wait!' I said. 'We are in good time for the boozer, let's turn back for a bit and see if we can spot it. If we don't,' I said, 'I will replace it.' I was not going to let anything stop us being happy.

So we turned around and slowly drove along the road the way we had just come. Five minutes, then ten, but just as we had it timed to turn back around and make a dash for the pub doors as they were being opened, we spotted a paper cup. Far ahead and on the opposite side, yes, there it was. But then, horror! A group of schoolboys was walking straight towards it, about fifteen yards off. I swerved across the road, and as I slowed right down to a crawl just a couple of yards from the cup, I opened my door leaned out and grabbed it just as the boys spied it. I held the trophy up and shouted, 'You missed this fifty pounds, lads!' As I waved it in front of them, it was pretty obvious they were thinking, 'how the hell did he spot that?'

We were now both laughing at our good luck in finding it. 'OK, Joe, let's head for Salford and Tommy Duffy's pub, the Railway, and for God's sake put it in your pocket this time,' I joked. We arrived back in town and got settled in Joe's favourite pub. I ordered two beers and we sat down at a table, but as I was drinking Joe was just sipping his beer a little at a time. 'Something wrong with the beer, Joe?' I asked him. 'No,' he replied. 'It's just that it hurts when I swallow, so I just sip it.' I had actually drunk three pints before Joe had finished his. 'I don't think I can drink another one,' he told me. 'I would like to go home now.'

I had never seen Joe like this before; he could normally drink ten or twelve pints easy. 'OK, I will take you home,' I said. But when he stood up he was very unsteady on his feet, so I helped him out to the car and took him home. Once inside, he slumped onto the settee. 'Joe,' I said, 'I think you should see a doctor, and quickly.' 'If I don't get any better, I will,' he told me.

The days and weeks rolled by. You could see the weight just falling off his once muscular frame, and eventually he went to see the doctor. After a lot of urgent tests it was confirmed that Joe had throat cancer. Of course he vowed to fight this massive problem.

The doctors told him, 'There is nothing you can do, you have three to four months to live. However, there is an operation that we can do, but the success rate is not very high. It's entirely up to you.' He chose to have the operation which they would do in two weeks' time.

During this time I visited him every day and sat by his bedside. I had to earn a living of course, so I used to pull up early morning outside his third floor window at the hospital, with a full load of tarmac on the truck, and toot the horn. I knew he would be up there looking out of the window, wanting to be with us to do his bit. He used to tell the other patients, 'That's my lad.' Not as a son, because he was my uncle, but as someone very close to him.

Then it was time for the operation. I was pretty naïve at the time, but my heart was in the right place. I suppose I did not know, or would not accept, just how serious this was for Joe. But he knew.

The operation was carried out and hailed as a success. The family went up to see him shortly after and he said, 'Lift me up, lads, I have slid down the bed and still have no energy to get back up.' All of our moods were jubilant, now maybe the food would stay down. As the visiting time was up, we all said goodbye to him and that we would see him the next day. Joe told us all in a happy voice, 'I think I have beaten it, lads.' You could see the relief in his face.

We all decided to stop on the way home and have a couple of beers, drinking to the good news we had just had. But, strangely, something was telling me not to drink so much, so I didn't. Early the next morning my phone was ringing; I was still in bed, it was that early. With trepidation I got up and answered it and, sure enough, it was the hospital. Joe had taken a turn for the worse, and could I please come as soon as possible to the hospital. Joe's family had already agreed that I would mostly sit with him at his bedside, so I phoned for a taxi and asked him to get me to the hospital straight away.

I was feeling very tearful and worried, what did this now mean for Joe? I guessed that they would tell me as soon as I arrived there. Walking down the long Victorian hospital corridors with smooth grey-painted concrete walls and no windows, the tears were flowing freely down my face. My heart was beating along with each one of my hurried footsteps, which seemed to echo in front of me. How many other people had trodden these same corridors and felt so much pain for their loved ones? My mind was racing, saying, 'Joe, please hang on. I will be with you soon, please hold on.' You could not run, you could only hurry and hope.

The corridor now turned sharply to the right, then it was all new glass and steel as it became part of the new extension to the hospital. All of the bright sunlight which wasn't wanted right at that time came pouring through. The hurt inside seemed to be getting a ray of hope, that maybe all was not lost; my emotions were in complete turmoil.

I entered the Intensive Care Unit. The nurses recognised and welcomed me, but I could hardly speak at that moment. One of the senior nurses asked me to follow her to the side office. 'Please sit down,' she said to me. 'I am afraid that I don't have good news. Your uncle had a very serious setback during the night, which does occasionally happen after such a serious operation, as we told you before. Your uncle appears to be fading fast, it seems like it is now imminent for him to pass away at any time. Would you like to sit with him for a while?' she asked. I told her I did and she brought me to him. I dried my eyes before I went, even though he could see no more, then sat by his bed and held his hand. He asked me in a quiet whisper, 'How do things look for me?' As he spoke those few words, the flooding of tears from my pained eyes wet my shirt. 'It's looking good,' I told him. This was the worst fucking lie I had ever told! 'You have beaten it,' I reminded him. Another rotten lie.

He lay there, his face a strange colour and sweating. I was talking to him, but there was no response, his power of speech was also gone. I now held both his hands and spoke softly to him, not knowing if he could hear or understand me any more. His life was fading fast now, ebbing away from this wonderful man who had helped save me from a very bad way of life. When I was a young man I had been pretty wild, but Joe had always helped calm me. Now all I could do for him was to speak very gently into his ear, telling him how I would always look after the family all I could. His wife was my aunty, his daughter was my wife. I wanted to ensure that the last thing Joe would hear in his life would be my quiet voice reassuring him.

Now he wasn't breathing, I watched the life and colour slowly drain from his face.

My tears did not matter to Joe any more, I knew he was gone, but he looked relieved now he had no pain. I stayed holding his hands for a while, then called a nurse over. 'I think he has gone,' I tried to tell her, but it came out of my mouth in a jumble and those tears would not stop. I waited while they confirmed that Joe had indeed passed away and then I left. I walked and walked, through the rain and the drizzle, where to I don't know, but slowly, and with a million thoughts in my head.

There was now no urgency for me to hurry anywhere. I headed towards home to the family. The tears subsided but the rain on my face and my red eyes appeared to make me look even sadder, they took one look and they knew without a word spoken.

As the days passed, Joe's funeral arrangements were well under way. A good friend of ours, Cathal Conlon, organised two beautiful Shire horses to pull the fine carriage that would hold Joseph Grundy's casket. Actually these two horses were famous. Those who remember the television advert for Webster's Yorkshire bitter, with the two talking Shire horses, will know which ones I mean. These horses were owned by a great man called Fred, who lived on a farm up on the side of the M62 Leeds motorway.

Joe had a wonderful send off, befitting a man of his stature. The travelling community came from far and near to pay their last respects.

The day we buried Joe was full of uncanny experiences. On the way to the cemetery two aeroplanes in the sky above us were giving off a smoke trail behind them. Coming at different angles, they made a perfect cross in the heavens. The two horses were called Uncle and Nephew, just like Joe and myself. Uncle stood upright and strong all day, which Joe was; Nephew was sad with head bowed, just like me. Joe's mass was held at St. Joseph's and he was buried at St Mary's, which is his wife's name. It was a cloudy day, but the clouds parted just long enough to make the horses' brasses shine as the photos were taken, like a glowing heart.

There were many signs that day and maybe, just maybe, Joe was looking down on us. RIP Joe Grundy, we love and miss you terribly.

The funeral of Joseph Grundy

John Boy, the New Boy in Town

John Boy was a new boy in town. Manchester was a new city to him, one that he had always wanted to visit. He had phoned me a couple of days earlier to ask if he could pull his caravan into the camp where we were staying. I told him it would not be a problem, he was welcome to come and stay. Although not related, I knew of John Boy. He usually travelled solely around Wales as he seemed to like that area very much, but he suddenly fancied a change so he came to visit us. A big enough man with a deep gruff voice, pushing fifty years of age, he had a wife and children to keep. Not one to cause any problems, he was welcome.

A very good worker, who always made a first class job of his tarmac, he would rather finish for the day if he had run short of materials and complete things the next day, rather than skim the tarmac on thinly just to finish the job. When John Boy and his family arrived, we made them welcome. 'I would like to buy you all a drink,' he told us. 'How about we wander down to the nearest pub?' Nobody said no to that, of course. There was plenty of chat from all of us, as we hadn't seen each other for a long time, so it was good to catch up on all the chit chat. We had close relatives staying where John Boy had just left, so we were able to ask him about their well being and so on. We had a good night.

As the days went by, John Boy asked if we minded if he looked for some tarmac work. 'Just to earn bread and butter money,' he told us laughingly. 'No, we don't mind at all. There's plenty of work in this area for all of us,' we told him. 'Can you tell me where this yard is that sells tarmac quite cheap?' he asked. We told him we would be going there in a few days' time, so if he wanted he could follow us there and I would introduce him.

A few days later, we all went to this yard for tarmac. We left at five in the morning as it was quite a long journey. I then introduced John Boy to the man on the weighbridge. This was the man who gave us a very good deal on the tarmac, with no receipt, but he was also making a lot of money for himself. Half an hour later, we were all loaded up and we left the quarry in good spirits. We had paid a very good price today, so profits from any work would be higher than usual, and that was how it was all that week. Happy days.

Come the following Monday morning, the only one to go for tarmac was John Boy. All the rest of us had been celebrating all weekend at a family christening. We had partied on for a long time, and were now the worse for wear. So John Boy decided to go on his own, as he wanted to get his work done. As he approached the yard, he did exactly as he had been doing all week. He parked up his truck, walked up to the weighbridge and spoke to the man through the hatchway. This was a little difficult because of the noise, as most of the drivers waiting for tarmac would leave their trucks ticking over, and – with the noise from the plant and machinery – it was difficult to make yourself heard here. 'Give me eight tons,' he shouted, for the third time. This time the man appeared to hear what John Boy said and wrote out a ticket and the bill.

John Boy looked at the price asked for and was taken aback. 'What the fuck's this price?' he shouted. 'No way, mate, I will pay you what I have done before.' The man told him, 'This is the price, mate, take it or leave it!' And again he asked for the full amount.

John Boy was now getting annoyed, he knew that this man was well clued up with the travellers and was now just taking the piss out of him. So he demanded, 'Give me the fucking tarmac, mate! There's your money, I don't have all day to fuck about with you.' At this, the other man in the office, who had been sitting there saying nothing and was supposed to be an office temp, walked over and said, 'I am a CID officer, and you are under arrest.'

The police were hiding around the rear of the building, and they swooped into this room and arrested the weighbridge man. 'What's wrong?' he shouted. 'I have done nothing wrong.' But the police officer revealed that they had been making tape recordings since the previous week. 'We know exactly what you have been up to. It is pretty obvious to us today that you knew something was up, so you were charging the right price,' he said. The company had apparently known that they were losing a fortune so they had called in the auditors who, after weeks of looking at the books, had called in the police. Quite a substantial amount of money had gone over the years, and they now knew that the man on the weighbridge, who had been a faithful employee for years, had been stealing vast amounts. He was placed under a caution and John Boy's details were taken.

The police initially interviewed the man at his home, then took him down to the nick where he squealed like a pig. He told the police that for years he had been threatened and bullied into giving out cheap materials to the travellers, and that he had made very little money out of it.

The statement to the police by this man pleased the police officers immensely, as travellers are the bane of their lives. If they could get to John Boy, they reckoned it would be a much easier case in front of the court. Blame the Gypsies, easy. They knew that John Boy had offered some payment for the tarmac, but of course it had not been nearly enough, so they arrested and charged him. The shock waves went through the travelling community, and we all spoke at length about John Boy and this massive problem while he was waiting to go to court. It was all bullshit, of course. We knew Dave, the weighbridge man, had been fiddling for years and had made a lot of money from this. He not only fiddled from the early morning, but on certain days he would also send out twenty ton loads with a private haulier if you had a big job on.

'Put the money in a sealed envelope,' he would tell us. 'When the driver delivers the tarmac to you, give it to him, and he will then bring it back to me.' Once the driver gave Dave the envelope he would receive a small percentage of it, while Dave kept the rest for himself. It would have been quite a substantial amount of cash off a big load like twenty tons. None of this, however, could be mentioned in court without any proof, so John Boy was the scapegoat for the massive amount of materials that had gone missing, and got two years in prison. Yet somehow Dave still kept his job.

We were all very shocked at what had happened to John Boy, so we all stayed out of that yard for a very long time. Dave was now being closely watched, he couldn't fiddle anything at all and now had to live on his meagre wages, which is what they were compared to the money that he had got used to. He couldn't leave the job, as that would have aroused strong suspicion about him even more. He was pretty sure the police were still trying to investigate his lifestyle over the previous few years, and still wanted to get him if possible.

He always came to work with a tan, which showed off his lovely white capped teeth. In those days there were no sunbeds, so we used to wonder how he did this, how he always looked so cool.

We found out one day, through a contact we had, that Dave owned an ocean-going yacht, and that he used to sail around Spain and the islands quite often. I bet the police didn't know this. We found out because he was now very hard up and couldn't pay his bills, so he had no choice but to sell the yacht.

In his heyday he was probably taking home much more than the top manager of the plant. Anyway, the boat went because he could not run it any more, and he was now finding it very difficult to pay the mortgage he had on his very large house. He had several big cars, but these were now going as well, sold off one by one to pay the bills. Of course, after several months, when his wife realised they would soon end up with nothing, she – like the boat and the cars – went too. She left him. So the fantastic lifestyle he had enjoyed for a long time had now slipped away from him. The busy social life, the parties, everything. He was now drinking a lot, and suffered bad bouts of depression. Things went downhill rapidly in

Dave's house, while John Boy was left to rot in prison. Dave only needed to tell the police the truth, that John Boy had only ever been to the yard for tarmac twice before, but the selfish bastard never did.

Finally, he lost the house as well. The mortgage company took it back, as he was behind on his payments with no hope of paying it off. By now Dave was drunk every day and he eventually got fired from the job that had given him such a great lifestyle through his fiddling, but in life all good things come to an end, as it did with Dave. Several months had passed by and one day a couple of us had a job to do not too far from the yard. We went in to buy tarmac. We didn't want to, but we did. We saw a new bloke at the office desk in the weighbridge. 'Where's that Dave then?' we asked him. 'Oh, he's dead,' the guy told us. 'What?' we replied. 'Are you sure?' 'Yes, he hanged himself a couple of weeks ago, it is his funeral today.' Just then three smartly dressed men came into the office and started to put their overalls on. I asked one of the men I knew by sight, 'Why are you dressed so smart, and now putting on overalls?' 'Well, Dave had worked here for twelve years, so the boss let us go to his funeral. Good job really, otherwise there would have been nobody there.' We just looked at each other. I said, 'Serves him fucking right!'

He let John Boy go to prison for two years, so he paid the ultimate price for being such a bastard to other people. As the saying goes... what goes around, comes around.

In Winston Churchill's Bed

I discovered a small airfield not far from where we had made a camp with our caravans. We had been very busy in the area with our tarmac, a lot of work had been completed, and I had put a few quid away as savings. I had kept on seeing all of these small light planes flying around and felt my adventurous spirit needed a boost. What better way than to fly a plane? I decided to go to the airfield to enquire if there were any flying lessons available and, if so, how much it would cost. They put me in touch with a small company there who did indeed give lessons, and were not too expensive either. They told me of a set price to guide me through to hopefully getting my pilot's licence, but I really wasn't interested in going all the way for that. I just wanted the buzz of being up there, to practise and then actually fly the thing. So I paid in advance for just two or three lessons at a time. Once you get into the plane at first you feel very nervous, but after a while you get used to it and settle down.

Six months before this I had been staying in Blackpool and had taken up the idea of a parachute jump. There are plenty of small airfields with loads of diving schools. So I thought, why not? It's really easy, you did some training, they took you up in a plane and then you jumped out – simple. Yeah, I'll have some of that. So I paid my money and signed up. We were all in a class, we all practised, had all of the usual mock-up jumps, learnt all the techniques of jumping and hopefully landing without breaking any bones. Then one day it was the real thing. There were seven of us doing a jump that day.

We took off in an aircraft, up through the clouds, and then it was level flight. 'Time to jump from the aircraft,' we were told. The instructor explained that we should make a line, one behind the other. I ended up sixth, with a young female going last behind me. Each person did exactly as they were told. 'Do not look down, and jump when told to.' One by one they stood on the narrow steel plate on the outside of the aircraft, looking straight in front of them. 'Jump!' the instructor would shout, and then they disappeared from sight. 'Easy,' I thought, 'this will be a doddle.' Now it was my turn. Gingerly I stood outside on the plate. The air was rushing at me. 'Hold your head up!' he shouted at me. 'And jump when I tell you.' I looked down, being a nosey bastard, but that is not the thing to do. All I could see down there were little white dots on a green background, they were sheep in a field.

I thought to myself, 'Fuck me! I am not going to jump from here, look how small the fuckin' sheep are, you can hardly see them.' Again he bellowed at me, 'Jump!' I had heard enough. 'Fuck off! You jump!' I shouted at him. My mind would not let me let go of that shiny chrome handle that I was holding onto as though my life depended on it. 'Come on now, lad, you can do this. Do not look down,' he said again. He was now trying the softly, softly approach, and I knew it. He had forgotten that I had paid for this stupid privilege to gamble with my life. 'Fuck you!' I thought. 'I have fought long and hard to look after this body of mine, and now this prick wants me to gamble with it.' All of my reasoning was gone. All this clown wanted was an empty plane, I was getting pissed off with him insisting I should jump.

The young girl behind me was still waiting patiently but very anxiously to go, so I stepped back into the plane and watched with admiration as the fucking nutter jumped out. I just looked at her as she floated gently down to earth. The instructor asked the pilot to throttle back a little so there was not quite so much noise in the back of the plane. Then he said again to me, 'OK, let's go for it now. Jump!' But I was not having any of it.

We eventually landed. As we left the plane, his mate walked up to him and asked if the trip had been a success. He started to mutter some excuse on my behalf about me not being steady or some shit, but I said, 'No, that's not true. I will not be so foolish to do that. I don't mind running and jumping from the police. But I won't when it's not necessary.' With that I walked off and I thought long and hard about whether I should cancel the cheque that I had given for this stupid idea.

And so back to the airfield and the flying lessons. Yes, it was a bit scary, but at least I was inside the thing without expecting to be tossed out.

No little steps and no handles, great. All I had to worry about was the joystick. I imagined that if I clenched it tight enough, it would stop us falling out of the sky.

After a few visits I got more confident with myself and realised I was quite good at flying a plane. The instructor was pleased with my progress and remarked that I seemed to be a natural pilot. I felt good about his words of encouragement. However, I did remark to him that it was like driving a JCB digger, and he looked at me incredulously, with disbelief on his face that I had said this. He could not tell if I was serious, winding him up, or just plain stupid.

But I was being serious. I am an excellent machine driver. When you fly a light plane it is all about a sense of touch, you build up speed, not much more than 65mph and gently lift this big lump off the ground with the nose easing up steady. Then a bit of extra lift as you are airborne, and off you go. Once you are up it takes no time at all to reach a decent height, level up and just fly. And then you need eyes like a shit house rat to make sure that you keep out of the way of any other Herberts that might be creeping up on you by mistake. Those are my words, not his, the instructor says, 'Be observant at all times.'

A JCB is a big machine, and yet if you treat it gently it will dig or lift any large object with just the smallest of revs. Using the levers gently, keeping the arm close, and easing the bucket underneath an object, you will do all you need to with a sense of feel. The principles are very similar. Both machines have plenty of power, and it is a pleasure to use them correctly.

We flew out to the Kent coast at first, following the line of the sandy beaches, then we headed back inland to base. After a few lessons, one day we were flying over the Dartford Bridge so we followed the River Thames along its snaking path into London. What a sight! It looks just like the picture at the start of EastEnders. The city is fantastic from up here, the London Eye, Greenwich Museum, the Arsenal Docks, the lot. 'We better turn now,' my instructor said, as we approached the Houses of Parliament, 'or we will become too much of a threat because of terrorism.' Blimey! Me, up here? I couldn't believe it. I was having the time of my life. I started to wish I was a wealthy man, as I would be up here night and day.

I started to enjoy the flying, I put in the hours on my logbook and soon I was taking off, flying in a loop, touching down and taking off again, all without stopping. I can seriously recommend this as entertainment.

After a couple of weeks' break, I realised one day that that was it. I couldn't spend any more money on it, it would have been just foolish. I had got my buzz, so all good things... as they say.

While flying around weeks earlier I had noticed a big mansion house in Kent. I was told it was called Chartwell House and that it had belonged to the late great Winston Churchill. This was a great man in his day, and I really enjoyed the sight, never thinking that he owned such a place.

Months had now passed by and we were steadily working away. We found ourselves in the beautiful village of Downe, tucked into the Kent countryside. As the labourers were getting on with the tarmac work one afternoon, I spoke to an elderly man outside a really old church. We chatted for a while and I mentioned Chartwell House. He told me that it was only a couple of miles away, and that if I was interested in history he would show me something. I was interested and I did have the time, so off we went. We simply walked a few yards into the graveyard of the church. 'Look at that giant oak tree,' he said as he pointed. 'Notice anything odd about it?' he asked. 'Not a thing,' I said. 'Well, it is nine hundred years old and the middle is hollow, through disease. Legend has it that one of the Kings of England was being pursued through here, chased by his enemies several centuries ago. In sheer desperation he jumped off his horse, shooed it away, and ran to hide inside this tree. His pursuers galloped past without seeing him and he was saved.'

We took a look inside the tree and it was massive; six people could stand with plenty space. If you stood with your back to the inside of the trunk and looked up, it was just open sky. The walls were no more than a few inches thick, and how it stands or supports such large branches is a mystery.

Also here Charles Darwin, that famous man from the Origin of the Species fame, has a plaque hanging on the church walls to commemorate his life. He had been a local man, who lived close by in a large house where he conducted his experiments, etc. He is buried in Westminster Abbey, with the great and the noble. In the graveyard is a headstone commemorating his faithful manservant's life, erected with gratitude for forty years of loyal service. 'You don't see that too often these days,' the old man said. I thanked him for his time and left.

After I had checked up on the men, I had to go and see Chartwell House, and took my grandson with me. We walked the grounds and entered the house. Magnificent, time seemed to stand still in this place. It was a real monument to a great figure. In and out of the rooms we went, then up the large stairs. We eventually found ourselves in the great man's bedroom, and then I saw the large four poster bed. Winston Churchill had actually slept here. I could not stop myself, right or wrong, and without thinking I put my grandson in his bed. Unfortunately the security men caught me doing this and went mad. But in all honesty, I didn't care what they said, it didn't matter to me. My grandson will always be proud to say that he had lain down in Winston Churchill's bed.

Getting It Too Easy
(The Mushroom Gang)

Looking around the caravans for a person who has a story for me to tell you about, there are maybe thirty odd to choose from. Then I noticed Jimmy the Bone.

He got his name through the size of his physique.

Jimmy is one of those people that never seems to worry. If he was skint you wouldn't know it, because he would always dress smartly and look good, never one to look down in the dumps. He could always come up with a pretty decent touch-up line to get a sub from you, one of them being, 'I have a load of work on but I cannot break into my money, it's for materials in the morning. So if you will lend me a bit I can repay you straight away once my work is completed.' And he would do this regularly then keep out of the way until he could repay. That was his gimmick. He wasn't hurting anyone and you never knew if he was telling the truth or not. He always paid up so that was it, good enough.

The amusing story starts like this. A warm and pleasant afternoon happened to be a Good Friday bank holiday, with the long weekend coming up. Jimmy had worked hard all week and had saved every penny for a good blast at the weekend. Plenty of booze and a good time was his intention. Not being married, he was going off down the town chasing the girls. And not being the prettiest of sights, he knew only too well the pulling power he had with a pocket full of money. First stop was Burton's for a new suit. 'Got to look the part,' he thought. Next, for amusement, he had to round up 'the mushroom gang'. These were his mates, all single and up for anything for a laugh. And finally, before they all met up, one last chance to get a good feed before all the drinking and partying started as it would be a long weekend for sure. 'It might last longer if the fun keeps up and the money holds out,' he thought to himself as he walked into a steakhouse.

Food ordered and eaten, and with phone calls made to 'the mushroom gang', Now it was close to the time to head off to paradise and into the arms of the first girl who would wear him.

Unknown to Jimmy, back at the camp one or two jealous eyes had followed his every move as he was busy doing his own thing. They had seen his stash, they knew what his plans were and they were eaten up.

'That little narrow cunt is going to spend all of that fine money on anybody at all in the next few days,' a couple of the men were saying. They had also worked very hard that week but with less success than Jimmy, and they had families to feed. They were also mad jealous that they could not join in and go and do what he could do; being single he had nobody to answer to.

Down at the pub 'the mushroom gang' had got together and instantly the party atmosphere started, the jokes – always new – the Irish blarney, the banter. No girl could resist the utter charm and boisterousness that these few had between them. Jimmy knew that by tagging along with these men, he would score with a girl during the weekend.

You could tag along, but to be a member of 'the mushroom gang' you had firstly got to be a traveller, secondly be very funny because this always got the girls in the happy, carefree frame of mind, and thirdly you obviously had to be single.

To join up with these lads, when they would let you, would make anybody's day. When they entered any pub the laughter was contagious. They should have been on the telly, they were so outstandingly funny. The only thing that they ever wanted was to be young, have a fantastic time with no responsibilities and a girl in every port, as they say. The travelling life was in full swing with plenty of moving from town to town, so a girl in every port seemed quite feasible.

When they would meet new girls, one of the many chat up lines was, 'Do you have any Irish in you, love?' To which most young girls would reply, 'No, I don't.' 'Well, you will have tonight, love, don't worry about that.' And this would be followed with great laughter from everyone.

I heard a bit of chat once that kept getting repeated several times, and I was mystified as to what was being said. It sounded like, 'My generals are waiting for you, love,' or 'my generals want a word'. After several enquiries with the gang, I found out that a girl had once remarked about a certain member of the gang's genitals, and the size. He had thought quite stupidly that she was praising his generals, so the word stuck, whatever it meant.

A young lady in the pub asked very quietly one evening about where 'the mushroom gang' name had come from. 'It's very simple,' the leader of the gang told her. 'It's best really that I show you, then you will understand better.'

So he called all the other members of the gang, including Jimmy, and asked them to form a tight circle around him, with the girl being in the middle. He said to the girl, 'Are you ready for this?' 'Of course I am,' she said. 'You can't embarrass me,' was her reply. Without further ado the leader of the gang unzipped his trousers and flashed, 'Look at the end of my dickie, it is shaped like a mushroom. This is what we are about.' With plenty of innuendo, this again was greeted with fits of laughter. When they weren't doing the serious stuff of real chatting up, there was always lots of foolery going on.

As was normal, whatever happened that weekend, happened. And then it would be basically forgotten.

The caravans were parked on the outskirts of Norwich town centre and it was now the middle of Sunday afternoon. The men were standing on this lovely, wide open grassy camp, when a most unusual sight appeared. A black taxi came in off the road and headed to where the men stood chatting. A lone figure was sitting in the back, skint, drunk and reading the News of the World newspaper. With his elbow propped out of the window, he just said, 'Anybody got a couple of quid for this chap?' then slid off the seat hiccuping. The men paid off the taxi for Jimmy and he staggered to his caravan and fell asleep. Two of the men standing talking were the envious ones, and they were seething. 'That is it!' said one of them. 'I am going to teach him a lesson.' They nodded to each other and walked off quietly.

A couple of hours passed and the heat of the sun, along with the beer, kept Jimmy conked out. The two men had made up their plan for Jimmy. They reversed a car very quietly up to the sleeping man's caravan, hooked it onto the back and drove off very gently. They took him and the caravan into the town centre, unhooked it and drove off and left him there fast asleep.

The honking of irate drivers' car horns did not stir our party animal, nor did the shouts of folk nearby.

As Jimmy awoke several hours later he stood up and went to the door. Desperate for a pee, he opened the door a couple of inches and let go with a sigh. He was just about to close the door when a big voice boomed out, 'And what the hell do you think you are doing then?' It was the police.

Jimmy froze. He had thought that he was still on a big grassy camp.

The police called him outside and there he saw what all the fuss was about.

He had been dumped in town alright, on a one-way system. Not only that, but this was the area where the ladies of the night got together. They were the ones that had been calling out in disapproval about the unwanted attention the caravan was causing to them and their punters. Luckily the police could see that he had not driven there, because there was no vehicle for towing. 'Get this thing shifted before I book you!' he was told. 'And don't you dare drive it away.' The officer had caught a whiff of Jimmy's breath and knew that he was well on it. 'Fuck it!' he thought. Jimmy being Jimmy, he went back to the pub he had left earlier, got a sub and left the lot where it was.

After a couple of hours the police were faced with the ladies, the punters, the added traffic, the dangers of an accident and so on. So they got a tow truck in. The caravan was brought back to the camp, which was funny, because the police only ever tow us OFF a camp, never back onto one.

Somebody gave Jimmy's details and he was left facing a big towing bill. The next day he was furious and tried to find out who was responsible, but no-one would say a thing. 'Well, fuck you all then!' he said as he walked off, thinking of his good times. It was all worth it, it was worth every last penny.

The Derby Fiasco

Stuart Street caravan site lies in the centre of Derby town on a small one-way system in the middle of a few factories, or at least it did when we stopped there. With a brick wall across the front, an opening in the centre for vehicles to get in and out, it was just a square plot of ground with enough space for five or six caravans to park on the left and the same on the right. A quiet site, half-empty, there was nothing out of the ordinary about this place until we pulled in.

Our gang can get on with anybody, a laugh a minute seems to be our motto. But after a week in Stuart Street, a trailer pulled in with none other than Mick the Liar and his wife and family. Everything was fine until Fat Jimmy got a phone call from his cousin. It was realised during this call that the last time we had all been staying together in Doncaster, after we had left and gone our separate ways in twos and threes, a dog had gone missing. A lovely brown and white lurcher, this dog was said to have caught every hare that it had ever chased. It was a really good dog. The dog had belonged to Fat Jimmy, and he was now being told that Mick the Liar had given a lurcher, with the same colouring, to his uncle. So Jimmy couldn't wait to clap eyes on Mick.

When they met on the campsite Fat Jimmy repeated what he had been told. Mick, being the biggest liar on the

planet, started to give his version of how it was nothing to
do with him and that he had never given his uncle any dog
of any description. 'Let's go down to the pub then,'
someone said, 'and we can get to the bottom of this.' And
with that we all took off walking out of the site across the
park and open grass land to the nearest pub in the town.
The walk, which we had done several times, took you
along a path which ran beside the River Trent. This area
was popular with the local folk as a place to relax and
maybe get a tan or read a book. The cross-examination of
Mick the Liar continued as we walked, and the evidence
seemed to be stacking up against him. The biggest thing
though that was going against him really, was his name.
Plain and simple, with a name like that, it had to be him.
With lots of accusations being thrown around, and lots of
previous misdeeds being brought up, tempers started to
rise. As we approached the river with its steep banks on
both sides, Fat Jimmy could take no more. And, with a
hard fling of his arm aimed square at Mick's jaw, he let fly.
Mick got caught flush and it knocked him into the river.
We all roared with laughter at the sight of Mick splashing
around, gulping for air as he called out obscenities at us all
for not helping him. We just carried on walking to the pub.
'I'm not going to listen to that lying bastard all afternoon,'
Jimmy said. As we left him further behind, we could hear
Mick going on that he couldn't swim. But that was just his
theatrics, anything for attention.

We entered the pub, ordered our beer and sat down,
getting stuck into lots of chatting about anything and
everything, but none of it concerning Mick. After a
couple of hours nobody noticed or cared that Mick had
not arrived. We reckoned he must have gone home to get
dried off and then decided to leave off the visit to the pub

today in case things got back onto him even more. As three o'clock in the afternoon arrived, we decided that we would head back home to the site and get some dinner.

As we walked back the way that we had come, we noticed a strong police presence in the park. 'There's something going on here,' we said to one another. And sure enough within two minutes of saying that, a bloke shouted out to the two officers next to him, 'That's him!' And he pointed at Fat Jimmy. 'What's your fucking problem, pal?' an innocent-looking Jimmy said to this do-gooder. 'He done it, he's the one, officer. I saw everything,' this person kept saying. And with that Jimmy's hands were handcuffed behind his back and he was marched to a waiting police van. 'What's the charge?' Jimmy was saying. 'What have I done? I've been in the pub all day with my friends, you have the wrong man.' 'Attempted murder,' came back the reply from the sergeant. 'No way!' said Fat Jimmy. 'You have definitely got the wrong man. Ask my friends, I have been with them.'

It was all explained to Fat Jimmy by his solicitor down at the police station, as he got two weeks remand in Leicester Prison, that throwing somebody who cannot swim into a river is indeed attempted murder. 'I'll fucking kill that lying bastard!' he screamed out. But that definitely didn't help when the officers repeated to the magistrates what he had said.

Fat Jimmy appeared in court two weeks later. Mick the Liar stood witness for him, explaining how he had obviously been accused in the wrong, as things were OK now, because the dog had miraculously found its way back home. The magistrates knew that things had been resolved and so they bound Jimmy over to keep the peace. Leaving the courthouse, the two looked at each other knowingly, shook hands and left it at that.

One Oak

We had seen enough of Derby for a while, so we all jumped onto the motorway and headed down south. We had decided to head any place towards London and check it out. The men gave Fat Jimmy a ribbing with, 'Hey, there are some great jails down here with stunning views, and the food is delicious.' The banter lasted all the way to Watford Gap.

Travelling around as a unit, the caravans are divided into certain categories. There are the family vans, the youngsters' vans for the teenagers, the workers' vans, and lastly the single men's or lads' vans, which are known laughingly as the 'Sallies', which is short for Salvation Army. You sometimes feel a little down and out living on your own in a Sally, even though the family are just feet away next to you. No clean socks on demand and stuff that you took for granted whilst 'at home'. You are also fair game for any relatives or friends who just happen to join up with the group, and who are male and single. You could have a bed all to yourself one night and the next there could be heads and feet everywhere. But when the fun starts, it is all well worthwhile. Things that you couldn't do at home, staying up late drinking or chatting, laughing, blaggarding, anything goes in the Sally.

Late one summer we were staying in the centre of some newly-built factories with the unusual name of

Nonsuch Trading Estate on Nonsuch Lane in Epsom, Surrey. Things were fine, the work was coming in and the camp was a good one. There was just one problem. Every time that one of us got pulled over and the police asked where we were camped, we told them 'Nonsuch place, mate, on Nonsuch Lane' and they thought that we were taking the Mickey. They had never heard of it. It only needed an awkward copper to bring you in for the night, so we felt that it was time to leave this place, as nice as it was.

Moving around Kent we eventually found our way to Sevenoaks, a beautiful old English town. Steeped in history and old buildings, it was – as the name suggests – originally built around seven large oak trees. The camp that we pulled into one evening was a tarmac road which was going to be the entrance to some new-build houses. Turning in off the main road it was a good few hundred feet long, and running down one side there was a grassy bank that was tree-lined. It was high at the entrance and tapered down as it followed this newly-laid road. At the end there was a turnaround circle, which was in a large open expanse. This was where the houses would go. We had all pulled in for the night. Some of the group just stopped their trailers as soon as they were off the roadway, some moved further down this new lane and some, to get more space, drove to the end and parked up in the wide open area. The Sally would always be parked away from the families in case of any late night antics. So on this occasion it was parked well in the open. Young Johnny Devaney, a bonny big stout lad, had joined the other three men in the Sally this night, which was nothing unusual. As the evening drew on, it grew ever closer to pub time. We set out to meet the neighbours in the local hostelry. The night passed by well and the locals had no problems with the new arrivals in their midst.

The evening drew to a close and we all made our way back home.

The wife and I and our three children were all in bed.

Everybody in the camp fell asleep, there was total silence as the last of the generators was switched off for the night.

First there was nothing, then a faint noise as we could hear people talking, becoming more frantic with each shouted message. Then we realised that something outside of our door was not right. It began to sink in that the voices were having big problems. When you wake from your sleep after drinking alcohol, it takes a few moments longer for things to register properly. The caravan was shaking, trembling, more forcefully as the minutes ticked by. The wife and I were now sitting on the edge of the bed taking it all in, holding our smallest child. A violent storm was upon us, the like of which had not been seen in this country for many, many years. We sat and listened to the commotion outside. Something told you not to go out unless you absolutely had to. Weighing up the situation, there were no vulnerable people in our group, elderly or on their own, etc, so it was better to stay put in case your own children were put in danger. As those long minutes turned into an hour and then two, the savage weather continued. The rest of the children woke due to the ferocity of the storm, the caravan shook and tilted and we huddled together. In a bleary state the night wore on. Eventually the noise outside subsided; it had been a scary night all round.

The following morning when I woke, it almost seemed like a dream. I stepped out and saw one family sleeping in the front of a truck. They had been awake all night and so afraid of their trailer turning over that they had spent the night in that cab. The trailers that were parked alongside the grass bank had been sheltered from the high winds. My trailer was on the slope of the bank, which had been only just safe, but my big ten ton truck had also acted as a windbreak being parked, by coincidence, in exactly the right spot. Further down the lane other families had tried in vain to turn their vans against the winds, but failed, and so had squeezed into each other's trailers for the night for safety. I don't know who had come off worst.

Johnny Devaney had stepped out of the Sally to go to the toilet right in the middle of the storms. We don't know if losing his body weight had made the trailer that bit lighter, or that a bigger gust of wind had come by. But, as he stepped outside, the wind lifted the caravan up off the ground. It turned over several times and came to rest in the middle of the surrounding fields, upside down. The three occupants that were sleeping inside were badly shaken up and needed hospital treatment. Johnny got hit with the front of the trailer, as it turned over. The front pointed bit that fits onto the tow bar caught his arm and broke it.

Calm followed and we were glad that it was all over. But later that day everyone soon realised that it might happen again that night. So the vans were brought up to the bank for safety, away from the open area. You have never seen so many caravans squeeze into such a small space. The Sally got left, because it was beyond repair.

A couple of nights later it was my wife's birthday, and it is the custom that we buy beer all night for whoever is there. We had everything in candlelight, which some might say is romantic, but to us it was simply the effect of the storm. All the power lines were down throughout the region, trees had been uprooted, and Sevenoaks had almost become Oneoak overnight!

Michael Fish, the BBC weather man, had made a famous quote the previous night saying, 'We have heard that there is a storm coming but don't worry, there isn't!'

We all decided to get back up the motorway, the quicker the better.

Being Approached.
My Big Fat Wedding

Eileen had just got back from the shops and had driven into the caravan site. There was a small crowd of young adults and children gathered around chatting like mad and smiling, an air of excitement was running through the travellers' camp like a virus. 'What's happening here? What's going on?' she asked her young daughter, Dolly, and the rest of the group. 'Has someone won the lottery?' 'Hi, Mammy, let me tell you what's happened and the good news for all of us.' She couldn't get the words out quickly enough and wanted to be the first to tell her mammy all she knew. Dolly was just eight years old, and could keep nothing to herself, no matter how private it was. She was always the one who seemed to know just about everything that was in the wind, but what she had to tell her mother was far from private.

'Mammy,' she started off, 'we were all playing games here when a very big posh car came into the caravan site and stopped by us. Some people got out and asked us where the adults were. We told them either out working, or shopping, so the man said he wants to put us all on the telly. And our Lizzy is getting married and they want to put her on the telly as well. And Mammy, you said I could be a bridesmaid, and Mammy, I will be on the telly as well, cause the man said I could be.' The words just tumbled out of the child's mouth without her taking breath; she was so excited.

'Now, Dolly, calm down,' Eileen told her daughter, 'and tell me again what all this is about – slowly.' Just then the rest of the women came back from the school run and were all asked to come and join this little party.

After listening to the children telling the story, the adults slowly managed to piece together most of what had happened. It appeared that Thelma, the dressmaker in Liverpool who makes all the dresses for the travelling girls' weddings, had somehow passed on the details of this next big Gypsy wedding and the very pretty bride-to-be Elizabeth, to the Channel 4 people. They had gone, 'Wow! This looks brilliant, we could make an extremely good programme from this.' Once the happy panic and furore had subsided, the women and children waited with baited breath for all the men to come home from work to see what their reactions would be. Of course, the afternoon took forever to go by because of this extraordinary event. The men returned home from work and, when all were present, they sat and spoke. Again little Dolly explained herself, enjoying the attention that was being focused on her. But this time, as she reached the end of the story, she pulled a badly crumpled-up piece of paper out of her pocket. 'What is that?' she was asked. 'I don't know,' she replied, as she was not able to read or write. 'Let's see,' said one of the onlookers.

It had a phone number on it and the words Producer and Channel 4. Nobody knew what Producer meant, but everyone had heard of Channel 4. They had seen it on the telly. Dolly continued, 'He said that he will come back in a few days, or else we can phone him.'

Everyone was now quiet, nervous and excited, nobody knew what to say or do. 'How can we phone?' they thought. 'What are we supposed to say?' They all agreed that it was a wonderful thing to be filmed on your wedding day, and to be on telly. The younger girls screeched, 'Oh My God, that is something else!' So with a general air of acceptance, it was left at that.

But not before too long there was great excitement again. The producers or members of their team had been back to Thelma's boutique and asked her to let them know when Lizzy was going to be in for her fitting, to try on the dress for size. They also asked if they could exchange phone numbers and meet with her to discuss the planned TV show. Acting as a go-between, Thelma did this. They all met at the local Pizza Hut for a spot of dinner, with the TV folk picking up the tab. The young girls with Lizzy were so over-excited they could hardly eat their food, squealing with delight at the thought of what was to come. This was glitz to them, this was glam, this was real Hollywood stuff!

Everything was explained to them about filming and when it would be on TV and so on. This was the biggest thing to happen to any traveller, ever. All the families were swept along with these events. They were minor celebrities, with the camera crews coming into the caravan sites and following them from caterers to cafes, and halls to hairdressers. Each of the programmes were an hour long, but the filming took much longer than this. They could have made a mini-Ozzy Osbourne-type series with the footage they took. Whatever fever took over at the time we don't know, but we kept seeing different film crews all over the travellers' sites in Salford and Manchester.

While they were filming us, we were also meeting up with film crews for several other documentaries, one of them being Danny Dyers' toughest men. There were also film crews from abroad – one lot was from Holland. 'We must be getting popular,' we said, 'or people are just very curious about travelling people.' This all happened very quickly, like a tidal wave of popularity. It just swept over us, and certainly none of us was in charge, yet we were the main topic of things.

The only thing ever given was a young girl's dream, and a few sequins.

And so that, as they say, was it. A blaze of popularity that netted somebody a fortune.

Getting ready for My Big Fat Gypsy Wedding?

Children playing as they were approached
by the TV people?

The Big Move

The wedding was over; the celebrations and the talking all finished. Who would be the first to mention Germany? We stood around the camp and each person was thinking the same thing.

Days earlier at the wedding reception, the buzz had been going around like a tornado. Go to Germany and earn your fortune.

'There are factory yards out there that are crying out to be done, no more little paths and house drives,' they were all saying. 'Nobody in all of Germany does any tarmacing, we will be the only ones. You get 30 Euros a metre for your work, guaranteed. This is treble the money you get here. You will be ordering a new Merc in three months, etc, etc.' Some voices pointed out that this was not like a trip to Ireland. 'It is a great voyage across Europe with foreign languages to overcome.' But once I heard this, I was hooked. Into the vast unknown – fucking hell, I love it!

Full of drink, Fat Jimmy, Johnny Devaney and I – well, just about all of us – had agreed to definitely go over and take a look to see if it was all true or not.

Now in the cold light of day, standing in the camp, we wondered if it was still on and who would mention it first. It was Michael who did, as he walked out of his trailer. 'Right, lads, are we up for it then?' he asked in an upbeat way. We looked at each other, and slowly the feeling came back over us. Yes, why not.

That was it, we got busy organising passports for anybody who didn't have one, getting motors serviced and ship-shape, and all of the other things that you would do if you were going on a long journey. We had heard that the food was different, some said it was crap, so we filled the cupboards with tins of beans and sausage, bacon grill and any other necessities. I can tell you some of those trailers with big families were severely overloaded. I'll bet we had two tons of beans between us; we wondered if we would get done for smuggling.

We set our sights to leave for the boat one week from next Monday. That gave us all plenty of time. I asked Manchester to come with us but he said no, so I got Jimmy O'Gorman and Black Michael – he got his name because he had jet black hair. I made sure that I was ready in good time and carried on drinking while everyone else got the last few things sorted. Sunday night before the big move, we all got together and double checked that things were in order. Some of the men brought other spare workers along to help.

Monday morning we were jumping like flies, itching to get onto the motorway for Hull docks.

We arrived, the tickets were bought, and we started to queue ready for loading. Men, women and kids were ecstatic. What an adventure, this was pure and total freedom. We make our own rules, we try to cause no problems, we live for work and our families; nothing could be better than this.

The basic words in German had been pounded into us from other travellers who had been there before. About seven words in total. 'I work on the motorway. I have plenty of spare asphalt.' That was it.

The logic was that if you say this to somebody and point at their car park that needs doing, they will then get somebody who can speak English and you can make a deal. Whole families, packed up and excited, were going into the unknown, and this was all anybody knew.

The workers, being bored, started drinking in the camp, they drank on the motorway, they drank while queuing on the docks, and they drank on board ship. By the time they were out to sea they were in oblivion. They got full value from the duty free shops with cigs and beers, 'just in case it was all a mistake' they told each other. As the night wore on for the gang, they ended up huddled at a table in a corner, speaking slurred, while the rest of us on board were partying and dancing in the disco bar. Jimmy O'Gorman got up to find the toilets. He had been before, but each time he came back and joined his friends he said that the toilets kept moving. The toilets were identical on board the ship, what he couldn't figure out was that every time he got up to go he turned left one time and eventually found the toilets, and next time he turned right and did the same. Having never left Ireland in his life except to go to England on a B+I ferry, this was a massive thing for him. Never had he been on such a large vessel or seen such things – restaurants, shops, hairdressers', cinemas and the like. 'There's even a room with a bar and a piano,' someone said in amazement.

On one late journey to the toilet, all hope of finding their cabins were gone and they stumbled on the Duty Free shop. Being late, the staff had walked off leaving it unattended. Our men walked past, spent up and very drunk. 'Let's have a look,' said one. In they trotted, stumbling with the sway of the ship and the alcohol. Picking up bottles they 'found' lying around and with nobody to stop them, they walked off with them for a few yards, found the toilet, went in for a pee and then sat outside on the carpeted floor and cracked open more fire water. The staff noticed the mess when they returned to their station and realised that the men that they had just walked past were the likely culprits. They had pulled cigarettes off the shelves, knocked cans and bottles over to get at what they wanted, and had convinced themselves that they would be back in the morning to pay, once they had got a sub off their bosses.

The captain didn't see it like that though. Standing over the men with his crew members, he could get no sense whatever out of these workers who were now on raw whisky straight from the bottle, passing it round and gulping it like cider. The men tried to explain, but it was useless. The bosses would pay but they were in bed in their cabins with their wives and children. When asked which cabins, these poor souls didn't even know their own cabin numbers. 'Right, that's it then. Lock them up!' said the captain. And that's exactly what they did. The cells on board ship are way down a staircase next to the engine room. You can shout all you want, but with the vibrating hum of the motors on the solid steel walls and doors, nobody will hear you. Once you are down there, you are history until the boat stops. As this all happened before the boat was halfway across the waters and still under British rule, the men were held below decks, sweltering with the heat, until the boat docked in the Hook of Holland. They were kept in those cells and returned back to England to face the magistrates and

British justice the following day. Those poor sods got off to a bad start.

'What a fucker!' we said. The men were needed, and we couldn't desert them. So we, the bosses, had no choice in the Hook of Holland than to spin a coin for who went back on that bloody ship, wait like a fool for it to dock back in England, get a taxi to the court, wait all day, pay the fine for the theft of a bottle of whisky – the rest of their haul was unopened – and then bring this dishevelled bunch back again to the waiting clan on the dockside. Nobody could move or dared to leave the docks for fear of getting lost.

We had begged the captain not to be so hard on us, but he wouldn't listen. 'I have had you lot on my ship before,' was all he would say. We found this funny, it cheered us up. Other men must have done the same or similar. Two-and-a-half days later we were all joined up. There was no laughing now, we were just pissed off wanting to get on our way. The women gave the workers a telling off for keeping them cooped up for such a long time with small children who had nowhere to play. Once we got out onto the autobahns though, it was all soon forgotten. A quick drive through Holland and in no time you are in Germany – yeah, here we go! Yahoo !

All of that morning and into the afternoon was spent driving. The progress was slow because we were wary of being on the opposite side of the road and it was also a very long drive. We were going to Bielefeld, some three hundred and fifty miles into Germany. We decided to pull over and have a rest in a service station for a while and grab a bit of dinner. During a conversation, with everybody listening, Fat Jimmy said to me, 'Well if we get the work here, there is no problem finding the tarmac yards.' We went quiet. 'How the hell had he figured that out?' we thought. We had not even realised that this could be a problem. 'How do you find a tarmac yard? Tell us, Jimmy,' we all said. 'What do you know?' 'Well,' he said, 'look at the turn-offs and they are all signposted.' Ausfart was on every exit sign. We did not know what it was, we could not pronounce it, but whatever it was it was obvious that when the same word was on every turn-off, it can only mean Exit. 'You thick prick!' we all laughed at him. He thought it said Asphalt.

Eventually we found our way to the town we were after. It was full of British Army lads, because there was a big barracks there. Fantastic! There were also plenty of shops selling everything you could possibly want, with food such as beans, HP beans, the ones that we had two tons of.

A funny thing happened one day. We had been there a few days and we were trying hard to pick up a bit of the language. We realised that really the first words you need to learn when going in and out of factories and hotels asking about resurfacing the car park, would be, 'Where is the boss?' So we were told that the German for this was, Ich bin cooken feer chef. I am looking for the boss. One of our lads, John, walked into a posh hotel and said this to the actual boss. The German bloke, realising that he was English or Irish, which is much the same to them, went into the kitchen and brought out the cook, thinking that this is what he wanted. He knew that chef in English is the cook, it never dawned on him that John was trying to speak German.

On the boss's say-so the cook willingly walked outside with John.

We sat outside in the car watching this. As John started walking around the car park pacing it out and measuring up, a cook in a tall white hat on top of his head started following him around, nodding his head to everything and agreeing. He looked over at us and said, 'What's so fucking funny, you lot?' That was it, we erupted into laughter, the cook started laughing as well. John went fucking mad. 'You are all a bunch of no-good bastards,' he said. He was upset and didn't know why. We couldn't tell him it was that funny, and he might strike out at somebody.

The end

The trailers pulled in en-route to Germany

Epilogue

What is a traveller? Is it a long-haired chap with a floppy hat and happy cigarette in his mouth? Standing around a camp fire while his friends chant away to the heavens and stars... Having left the security of 'mummy and daddy' in their smart semi, while he goes on another regular summer jaunt to Stonehenge and the like, all happy and carefree, meeting with friends from previous adventures, a brush with the law here, a broken down van there, sign on in different towns. This New Age travelling is fun...

Today's travelling people have nothing against this.

The great potato famine of 1845, which lasted over two years, killed over one million people in Ireland. With no work through the blight, there was no money. Two years is a mighty long time; folk were evicted from their homes because the rent wasn't paid. Starvation ruled supreme. In time starved corpses lay rotting, mothers cried over their babies and proud men, resigned to their fate, prayed for an end to this human purgatory. With the most basic of things – FOOD – not available in those extremely poor times, things were dire.

On a nationwide scale, it was almost similar to Hitler's worst efforts. A further one million escaped all of this and resettled elsewhere. These are massive numbers for an island so small. The country took many,

many years to get over what happened, as further smaller problems slowed down progress. My people left Ireland at the turn of the century. To pay for their tickets (it is alleged) a couple of horses went missing. In those days rustling was a hanging offence, but things were desperate at that time.

Anyhow, true or not, they found their way to these shores. Some settled in Wigan, others in Manchester. My great aunt Alice married into the Sheridans, aunt May married into the Yorkshire Cunninghams. Others of our clan went to Scotland, where there is a large family group to this day. So why do I divulge this non-important message?

The travelling life was fine throughout the years, the good and the bad. As the Eighties drew in, first small groups of New Age travellers appeared on the scene, and then later on they became huge convoys. They attracted the TV and the media, etc, and things came to a head. A group of MPs decided that all the ancient heritage sites were getting trashed on a regular, organised basis. The answer that they came up with was simple, the outlawing of no more than five "travellers" vehicles in convoy at a time, and they gave power to the police to move anybody on who pulled in for the night.

These laws were pushed through Parliament quickly during the last day of business before the Easter break. Who wanted to pore over paperwork over such a trivial matter? Nobody. So it was passed.

The wording meant the end of our way of life as it was. Unintentionally, yes, but it was there in black and white. It didn't affect us straight away though. It was only when travellers pulled into a town where they weren't particularly wanted that the local police realised these new laws could be used. And, believe me, there were some instances where this extra power was used to its full extent, and at some very bad times of the day, with rain pouring down or night time when you were desperate to put children to bed or get fed. As the end justifies the means, it was this series of actions that made lots of people go out, buy a piece of land, move their caravans onto it and then apply for permission to live there. We didn't want it this way; people sometimes could not afford to do this, but it was necessary to survive.

One day, while at a funeral in Ireland, we went to the pub to toast the life of the poor departed soul and I was asked if I was interested in a piece of ground in England. I thought about it. Being in Ireland, there might be a catch, but what the hell! I had been looking for somewhere and was finding it tough. Even though I always liked to be on the move, my grandchildren were going to need some place to live in the future. So I asked my friend the price of the land. I could afford it, just. 'Before I buy, I have three questions,' I said. 'Is the land a soft bog or solid?' 'Solid,' he replied. 'Is it going up the side of a mountain?' 'No,' came back. 'Well, is it going down the other side then?' The pub had been listening and erupted into laughter at this. Again, 'No,' I was told. And with those words the deal was done. Such is the quick way things are completed when you want something.

And so the politicians have inadvertently made me become a landowner.

A Last Word

How many giant leaps can you take in one lifetime?

To escape dire poverty and famine, legend has it with us that several horses went missing to pay for boat tickets away from all the starvation.

Horse rustling was a hanging offence in those days. The penalty was overlooked, the chance was seized, and we as a family went into the unknown and headed for England. A giant leap!

Once all of England and Wales and Scotland had been travelled,
it was off again. Another leap.

Off into the unknown and into Europe, all of it.
Spain, Austria, Luxembourg, Norway and Denmark. A bigger leap.
Then, to cap it all off, we ended up in the USA and Africa.
A massive leap.
Oh, and not forgetting our time in Australia. A monster leap.

We have worked our way through the lot.

Our next book *GYPSY and TRAVELLERS'
TALES... EUROPE* includes:

- Snowball fights in Kloisters whilst Prince Charles is
  holidaying there*
- Getting lost up the Eiffel Tower*
- Playing on Robert Maxwell's £35m yacht in the
  South of France*
- Flying a plane over Berlin,*
- Paddy's day in Potsdam*
- Total chaos in Sweden*
  And much, much more.

The stories are funny enough but, with the language
barrier, some of the situations turned into non-stop
mayhem.

This book in no way sets out to give a view of
travellers' or gypsies' day-to-day lives. It is one man's
journey through life that is meant for entertainment
only.

I hope that you have enjoyed this read, as I have enjoyed
telling my memories, and look forward to sharing our
European adventures with you next time.

Alexander J Thompson.